THE FERRY STEAMERS

THE STORY OF THE DETROIT–WINDSOR FERRY BOATS

1938 Windsor and Detroit ferry tickets.
– AUTHOR'S COLLECTION

The ferry HALCYON taking on foot passengers and vehicles at the Walkerville dock around 1941.
– WINDSOR STAR PHOTO

THE FERRY STEAMERS

THE STORY OF THE
DETROIT–WINDSOR
FERRY BOATS

Stoddart

WILLIAM OXFORD

A BOSTON MILLS PRESS BOOK

PUBLISHED WITH THE FINANCIAL ASSISTANCE OF THE ONTARIO HERITAGE FOUNDATION,
ONTARIO MINISTRY OF CULTURE AND COMMUNICATIONS

To my wife Joyce and my family

Canadian Cataloguing
in Publication Data

OXFORD, WILLIAM.

  THE FERRY STEAMERS

Includes bibliographical
references and index.

ISBN 1–55046–078–1

1. Ferries – Ontario – Windsor
   – History.
2. Ferries – Michigan – Detroit
   – History.
3. Windsor (Ont.) – History.
4. Detroit (Mich.) – History.
I. Title

HE5785.W5509   1992
386'.6'0971332   C92–095625–4

Design and Typography by
Kinetics Design & Illustration
Printed in Canada

First published in 1992 by
Stoddart Publishing Co. Limited
34 Lesmill Road
Toronto, Canada
M3B 2T6

A BOSTON MILLS PRESS BOOK
The Boston Mills Press
132 Main Street
Erin, Ontario
N0B 1T0

The publisher gratefully acknowledges the support of the Canada Council, Ontario Arts Council and Ontario Publishing Centre in the development of writing and publishing in Canada.

The Walkerville ferry waiting room and exit from the custom pens around 1930.
— WINDSOR STAR PHOTO

Front Cover: The Ferry PLEASURE
— THE DETROIT NEWS

Back Cover: The BRITANNIA was initially built in 1906 for the Detroit – Belle Isle run and did not enter into regular ferry service until 1926.
— WINDSOR STAR PHOTO

TABLE OF CONTENTS

PREFACE

ONCE UPON A TIME, in the not-so-distant past, there were ferry boats on the Detroit River. Like the trolley cars on city streets, the steam locomotives, and the five-and-dime stores, they have vanished from our midst, becoming another chapter in the colourful history of Windsor and Detroit. For many readers of this book, mention of the ferries will bring back memories of pleasant summer evenings crossing the river on a boat's upper deck, or stopping for a cream Vernor's at the foot of Detroit's Woodward Avenue, or patiently waiting for the next boat to arrive on a bitterly cold day in winter. I am speaking of a time when sturdy little ferry boats steamed constantly back and forth across the Detroit River, keeping pace with the two communities they served. Quite a few of them had wonderful, even exotic, names, which are still easy to remember: WALK-IN-THE-WATER; TASHMOO; GREATER DETROIT; CADILLAC; LA SALLE; ARGO; ESSEX. Who could forget those graceful steamers? They were like family, familiar, lovable, and central to our daily life.

The ferry business began very simply. When settlers on either side of the river wanted to cross to the opposite shore, they usually hired a skilled oarsman to take them, unless, of course, they used their own boat to ferry themselves. And the business did not end until well into its second century in the face of insurmountable competition from the Detroit River Railroad Tunnel (1910), the Ambassador Bridge (1929), and the Detroit-Windsor Tunnel (1930). The last named was for vehicular traffic.

My purpose in writing this story is really twofold: to give my generation a look back upon our past, and to give present and future generations a glimpse into that part of our life affectionately referred to as "the ferry era".

This book spans a period of approximately 150 years during which Canada and the United States experienced vast changes as they grew from basically rural societies into complex industrial nations. Concerning Windsor and the province of Ontario, I would like to make two points:

1. The settlement located on the south shore of the Detroit river, the future site of Windsor, was initially called "South Shore" or "South Detroit". The local French inhabitants named the area "La Traverse", a crossing place. In later years, due to the ferry traffic to and from Detroit, what is now downtown Windsor became known as "Sandwich Ferry", "Ferry House" or just "Ferry". As business increased, the community around the docks expanded. Soon the inhabitants were looking for a new name. "Richmond" came into common but unofficial use. In 1834, there was a public debate over which name to choose, "Richmond" or "South Detroit". Neither one seemed to satisfy a majority of the locals, so an entirely new name was adopted, "Windsor", which has remained to this day. For the sake of simplicity, I will use "Windsor" to identify the Canadian side of the river, including Sandwich and Walkerville, regardless of the year. Windsor was incorporated as a village in 1854, as a town in 1858, and as a city in 1892.

The WALK-IN-THE-WATER, shown here at the foot of Third street in Detroit, was the first steamboat in the Windsor-Detroit area.
– WINDSOR STAR PHOTO

2. Prior to 1791, the territory in which the settlement of Windsor lies was part of the old province of Quebec. After that date, the western portion of the province became Upper Canada. On 10 February 1841, by virtue of the Act of Union, Upper and Lower Canada were united as Canada West and Canada East into the Province of Canada. In 1867, the Province was divided into Ontario and Quebec. During the period leading up to Confederation, however, the old names of Upper and Lower Canada survived in popular use and sometimes appear in official documents. It is important for the reader to keep these historical distinctions in mind, and to realize that I am talking about the same territory when I speak of Upper Canada (the western portion), and the Province of Ontario.

In conducting my research, I examined books, theses, articles, and newspaper stories. I also made personal contact with a number of people who remember the ferries as I do and who share my love for the steamers. Memories are personal, however, and it is usually only the good feelings we recall, not necessarily the specifics of any given year or boat or incident. Lastly, I came across many conflicting pieces of information, especially with respect to dates. I have done my best to choose the date and information that seemed most likely to be correct. Any mistakes, of course, are my own responsibility. I ask the indulgence of my readers, and invite them to enjoy this history of the ferry boats.

W. OXFORD
April 1992

ACKNOWLEDGEMENTS

For a first time author the gathering of material for this book seemed overwhelming and indeed would have been but for the generous assistance I received from so many individuals and organizations, and to all of these I am indeed thankful.

I am especially grateful to the Windsor Public Library for their patience and their assistance as I sat month after month at their film readers gathering data from old newspaper records. I am grateful also to Mr. Mark Walsh and the staff at the Windsor Municipal Archives, the Detroit Public Library, the Hiram Walker Historical Museum, the Great Lakes Historical Museum (Ohio), the Windsor *Star* and the Essex County Historical Society, and finally the Ontario and National Archives of Canada. Each of these organizations gave me free access to their files and permission to use photos held in their collections.

Many individuals also gave me a great deal of support and assistance. After I moved to Midland, Malcolm Campbell, Stan Goldspink and Ray Barnes supported the project by doing my legwork in Windsor. Bill Ransome (Amherstburg) dug into his files of historical data and found not only ferry information, but a couple of original Detroit and Windsor Ferry Co. tickets. Don Wilson (Windsor) graciously permitted me to use two photos from his extensive post card collection. There were others too who shared with me their personal memories, and these I have included to illustrate the lighter side of the ferry boat story.

I would like to give a special thanks to Michael Power (Windsor historian, now living in Welland), who not only took on the enormous task of editing the manuscript, but contributed to the story from his own vast knowledge of Windsor's history. I am grateful as well to the Ontario Heritage Foundation for their financial support in publishing this book.

Finally, I am very grateful to my family who gave me so much encouragement, and especially to Doug Stockton, who gave so freely of his computer time and expertise. To all of these I simply say thanks.

W. OXFORD

The "Showboat" dance pavilion (c. 1948), featuring Claire Perrault's orchestra, was once the thriving ferry docks in Windsor.
– WINDSOR STAR PHOTO

The BATEAU was an early type of vessel used on the rivers and lakes. The boat pictured is located at the Historic Naval and Military Establishment in Penetanguishene Ontario.
— AUTHOR'S COLLECTION

CHAPTER I

IN THE BEGINNING

1800-1830

On a warm and sunny day, in the summer of 1938, the border cities of Detroit, Michigan and Windsor, Ontario played host to one of the largest and loudest celebrations in their history. Early in the day, small clusters of people began to congregate near the ferry docks on both sides of the Detroit river. By late evening, the number had swelled into the thousands. The merrymakers had gathered to bid a boisterous yet sad farewell to their old and trusted friends, the ferry boats. The Detroit and Windsor Ferry Company had ceased to be profitable since the opening of the Ambassador Bridge and the Detroit-Windsor Tunnel. The company was closing its doors on Monday, 18 July 1938.

To the thousands jammed on the docks that day, it seemed that the ferry boats had been running forever. No one could remember the river without the passenger ferries. Their parents, even their grandparents, had often spoken of taking trips to the other side. After this day, however, the boats' familiar whistle, sounded as they pulled away from dockside, would be silent. The waiting rooms and car pens would be empty. The ferries themselves would sit idly in the water until they were sold to the highest bidder. The imminent demise of the ferry system drew quite a crowd to the river for one last crossing and perhaps for a few souvenirs to take home. Many, unable to board the vessels, stood on shore to watch and cheer every time a ferry, its decks fully loaded, started to make its way to the opposite dock. Others stood quietly, savouring their own memories, and among these people there must have been quite a few whose thoughts turned to the earliest ferry boats. When did the ferries begin to take people across the river? What were the first boats like?

During the latter portion of the eighteenth century, when the two communities were still largely French Canadian and little more than a series of family farms and a collection of wooden buildings along the banks of the Detroit river, bateaux were the principal means of passage along or across the river. A bateau was specifically adapted for travel on the great lakes:

> The bottom of it was perfectly flat and each end was built very sharp and exactly alike. The sides were about four feet high, and, for the convenience of the rowers, four or five benches were laid across, according to the length of the bateau. It was a heavy sort of vessel for either rowing or sailing, but preferred for the reason that it drew little water and carried large loads, and was safer on lakes or wide rivers where storms were frequent. The bateau was at times propelled by means of sails, oars, and poles.[1]

Over the winter months, when the river was frozen, the bateaux were naturally unable to operate. People crossed on foot, on skates or by sleigh. Brushwood was piled high at intervals marking the safest route. Travelling in this fashion was fairly safe during the daylight hours and on moonlight nights at the height of winter. The ice, though, was always a problem. It was not uncommon to hear of people losing their way or drowning. The following item from the parish records of Assumption Church in Sandwich, dated 1 January 1785, tells one such story:

> Menard, wife of Belair, was drowned with Demer's daughter while crossing the ice on a cutter. Demer's wife, who held her one-year old child in her arms, was rescued by her husband. Belair and Duroseau hung on to Demer's cape and were also rescued.[2]

Life in both communities changed in 1796, the year the British evacuated Detroit in compliance with the terms of Jay's Treaty. The administration of the Western District (the forerunner of Essex, Kent, and Lambton counties), was removed to Sandwich, where government officials and their families settled. For those British subjects who had businesses and homes on the American side, they were allowed to keep them and travel freely back and forth. Up until 1796, communication between the north and south shores was relatively infrequent. This changed with the transfer of Detroit to American authority. Ties of kinship and business increased river crossing traffic, and, correspondingly, the need to ferry people from one side to the other on a regular basis.

Within a very short period of time, traffic on the river had increased sufficiently for the Americans to inaugurate a system of ferry owner licenses. The Court of General Quarter Session was the regulatory body. It issued its first license to John Askin (1739-1815), one of Detroit's wealthiest merchants and most successful fur traders. Dated 1 February 1798, it was signed by Winthrop Sargent, then acting governor of territory northwest of the Ohio River:

> Be it known to whom it may be concern: that John Askin, Esquire, of Detroit in the county of Wayne having applied for a licence to keep a ferry from the landing of the shore of the river Detroit, I have thought it to grant the same for and during the term of one year from the date hereof and do by these presents authorize and empower him, the said John Askin, to ask, demand, and receive from all persons he shall transport across the water, and for all horses, carriages, and cattle of every kind such rates and sums of money as are used to be taken. Enjoining upon, and requiring of him that when the Court of Quarter Sessions shall establish the rates of ferriage, he shall exactly conform thereto, and also to provide and keep food and sufficient boats and the proper complement of able and skilful persons at all times in readiness for the transportation of passengers at reasonable hours in the daytime, otherwise this license to be void.[3]

Although not much is known of Askin's ferry business, any success he had may be measured by the desire of others to be licensed. A license was granted to an English immigrant, Gabriel Godfroy, on 5 March 1802, to operate a ferry from his home in Windsor to the foot of Woodward Avenue in Detroit. Godfroy charged one shilling per passenger for his services. Thomas Askin received a license on 7 December 1802. He was followed by James May, 21 December 1803, and Jacob Visger, 9 July 1804.[4]

François Labalaine (Leblaine?) was one of the pioneer French Canadian ferrymen. He lived near the old Janette farm, in the vicinity of present day Janette Avenue and River-side Drive West. In his memoir, *Souvenirs of the Past*, William Lewis Baby tells us that Labalaine had been a fur trader for the Hudson Bay Company in his younger years.[5] Rheumatism ended his career with Hudson Bay, but it did not stop him from taking up a second and more leisurely profession. This "old and honourable servant" of the company ran his ferry from a point near his home to four different landings in Detroit: Woodward Avenue, which was the most popular spot, Griswold, Shelby, or Cass Streets, depending on the wishes of his customers. For a round trip he was paid the equivalent of twenty-five cents in modern money. Labalaine was full of stories of his days in the Northwest Territories. He loved to talk about his life among the Indians and his fellow fur traders. A trip with Labalaine at the helm could be most entertaining. In addition to his story telling, he was usually inclined to sing a song or two. His one fault was to linger on the American side and swap stories with the dock hands and loafers. Quite often he was not available when a client appeared at his home. Baby recalls that Labalaine's wife was a very patient woman who knew her husband's habits all too well. She kept a four foot tin horn outside the front door of their home by the water's edge, and she wasn't too shy to use it. She would blow a mighty blast to get his attention. It was his cue to return home immediately. Business was waiting!

Labalaine apparently owned a log shaped canoe. He was not the only one. Pierre St. Amour, proprietor of a small hostelry at the northwest corner of what is now Ouellette Avenue and Riverside Drive, was another log canoe ferryman, at least in his early days in the business. He took out a license on 11 January 1820, primarily for the convenience of his guests.[6] The location of St. Amour's tavern appears on the 1835 map of Richmond. It survived the great fire of 1849 (as did the Windsor Castle), and it was succeeded by the British North American House.[7] When Labalaine started ferrying people across the river, South Detroit consisted of his hotel, Moy Hall, built in 1799,[8] and a few farm houses. Within fifteen years, the settlement grew considerably. By 1835, it consisted of no less than forty-six stores, residences, and warehouses. St. Amour's family was still in the hotel and ferry business, his widow living at a separate dwelling on the same property, but they had some competition. A man known as Ferry Master Mclean ran the Pig and Tinder Box Tavern and Ferry on the site of Labalaine's old stand.

At some point in time, even William Baby, St. Amour's neighbour, became involved in providing passenger service to and from the Canadian shore. He pulled together a small fleet of seven rowboats, hired men to row them, and added a scow to his fleet for the conveyance of teams of horses, cattle, and large groups of people who wanted to attend reunions or picnics.

In John Askin's 1798 license, "rates of ferriage" were to be established at some future date by the Court of General Quarter Sessions. The court fulfilled its intension by issuing its first "Regulations for Ferries" on 9 December 1802: "Detroit River in Winter- from 1st of November to 1st of April, Man,1-s, 6-d (1 shilling, 6 pence): Horse, 4s. In Summer – 1st April to !st of November, Man 1-s: Horse, 3-s.[9]

More specific and detailed regulations were issued by the American authorities in 1820:

Each Ferry shall be provided with two sufficient and safe canoes or ferry boats, and one sufficient and safe scow or flat. From the first day of April until the first day of November in each year, each ferry shall be attended by two good and faithful men, and from the first day November to the first day of April by three like good and faithful hands. The ferry shall be kept open from the rising of the sun until ten o'clock at night, and at all times, when practicable, shall transport the mail and other public express.

The rates of ferriage shall be as follows: From the first of April to 20th of November, for each person, 12-1/2 cents; for each horse, 50c.; for a single carriage and one person, $1.00; for each additional person, 12-1/2c.; for each additional horse,25c.; for each head of horned cattle, 37-1/2c.; for each sheep or hog, 6-1/4c.; from the 20th of November to April 1st, for each person, 18c.; for each horse, 75c.; for each single horse, carriage and one person, $1.50; for each additional person, 18-3/4c.; for each head of horned cattle, 56-3/4c.; for each sheep or hog, 9c.[10]

Several things about these regulations call for some comment. One, the initiative to regulate the ferry business came from the Americans. The response of the Canadian officials was for the most part negligible and probably limited to following the American lead. Two, the business had obviously grown to include large numbers of people and a steady trade in livestock between the two countries. The ferries were crucial to local economic growth. Indeed, they would become vitally important to the economy of the region once the Talbot Road, the Erie Canal, and the first Welland Canal were completed, linking the eastern seaboard, upper New York State, southern Upper Canada, and the American midwest. The connection at Windsor and Detroit was already decisive as early as the 1820s.

The landing at Woodward Avenue gradually became the centre of activity along the Detroit shoreline. One American bar owner who was upset at this development was "Uncle Ben" Woodworth. He was losing valuable customers from his bar at the Steam Boat Hotel. He decided to open his own ferry service, which would leave from the foot of Randolph Avenue, next to his establishment, and stop at Brock Street in Windsor. Confident of success, he advertised his service in the Detroit *Gazette*, 20 April, 1820:

OVER! OVER!
The subscriber has obtained a licence to keep a Ferry on the Detroit river, and calls on the public for patronage. He has provided an excellent Flat, and his Boats for passengers are superior to any that can be found on the

Pierre St. Amour, an early ferry boat operator, also kept a hostelry at the corner of Ouellette Avenue and Sandwich street.
– Windsor Star Photo

Mrs. Labalaine kept a four foot horn beside her back door to summon her husband home from the opposite shore when customers were waiting.
– Author's sketch

Horses were used to power ferry boats in the early eighteen hundreds. This horse ferry is typical of the type used on the Detroit river.
– Windsor Star photo

River. Careful men have been engaged to attend the Ferry, and constant attention will be given, in order that passengers may suffer no delay. Persons wishing to contract for their ferriage by the year, will be accommodated at a low rate, and landed at any point within a reasonable distance of the landing-place on the opposite shore. Freight will be taken over at a low rate. The Ferry is kept nearly in front of the Steam Boat Hotel.

B. Woodworth

N.B.– Persons wishing to cross are desired to give notice at the Steam Boat Hotel.[11]

In 1825, a new type of ferry boat made its debut on the river. It was powered by neither man nor wind but by horses! John Burtis and D. C. McKinstry heard of a "horse boat" being built in Cleveland. Realizing the growing potential of the ferry business, they went to investigate and ended up buying the "horse boat" and bringing it back to Detroit. As soon as they had their license, they took out the following advertisement in the *Gazette*, 22 September 1825:

HORSE-BOAT FERRY

The subscribers have recently acquired a large and commodious.

HORSE-BOAT

for the purpose of transporting across the Detroit river, passengers, wagons, horses, cattle, etc. The boat is so constructed that wagons and carriages can be driven on it with ease and safety. It will leave McKinstry's Wharf (adjoining that of Dow & Jones) for the Canadian shore, and will land passengers etc. at the wharf lately built on that shore by McKinstry and Burtis. The ferry wharfs are directly opposite. Mr. Burtis resides on the Canadian shore and will pay every attention to those who may desire to cross the river.

D. C. McKinstry– J. Burtis[12]

The boat, which was named the OLIVE BRANCH, was essentially a highly modified scow. It had two immense paddle-wheels amidship. Connected to them by shafts, and flush with the deck between them, was a large circular table on rollers with radiating spoke-like ridges. Upon this table and directly opposite each other were harnessed two strong French ponies. As the ponies walked, the table revolved, and thus the paddle-wheels were set in motion. At fifty feet long and thirty-two feet wide, it was an attraction on the river. Friend Palmer remembered seeing the OLIVE BRANCH in the early summer of 1827:

After passing by Sandwich (on the steamer from Buffalo), the first sight that greeted us was that of the Windmills — three on the Canadian side and two on the American side. On nearing the Detroit a more interesting sight was that of a horse-ferry boat, Captain John Burtis, running between Detroit and the Canadian side. It was propelled by a horse walking around in an enclosure which looked like a large cheese box on a raft.[13]

Despite its many advantages, the boat proved to be a financial failure. In 1829, Burtis and McKinstry lost nearly four hundred dollars.[14] They continued to operate it for several more years, then sold it to Pierre St. Amour. He had it refitted and with a bout of optimism issued this notice:

The public are informed that the horse boat has been thoroughly repaired, and will ply regularly between Detroit and the opposite shore. The decided advantages of this conveyance over the sail ferry boats will readily occur to all, and it is hoped that the liberal patronage which it has heretofore received will not only be renewed, but increased. The boat will leave the foot of Bates Street every half-hour during the day, and every exertion will be used to accommodate and please.[15]

The HORSEBOAT lasted a few more years, but it was soon eclipsed by the introduction of the steam driven ferry.

The ARGO, the first steam ferry boat on the Detroit river.
— Windsor Star photo

CHAPTER II

THE ARGO

1831-1835

Denis Papin is generally credited with building the first steam powered boat, around 1707. It was another century, however, before Robert Fulton constructed what is considered the first commercially viable steam powered vessel, the CLEARMONT. Fulton's vessel plied the waters along the east coast in the vicinity of New York City and up and down the Hudson River. Its success ushered in the era of the steamboat. It was approximately 1817 when the first steamer, WALK-IN-THE-WATER, made its debut on the Great Lakes. It made stops at various communities along Lake Erie and the Detroit river, and it even visited different locations on the upper lakes. Soon she and other steamers were a familiar sight.

John Burtis, the man who introduced the horseboat to the Detroit river, built the first steamer to work the Windsor-Detroit corridor. Called the ARGO, it was a side-wheeled boat assembled by Detroit Drydock Company at the foot of Riopelle Street. Opinions differ over the exact year the ARGO was put into service, and where she first worked. Two dates have been given, 1827 and 1830. Some sources favour 1827 and make the claim that the ARGO was initially used on the St. Clair river and then brought to the Detroit river in 1830. Anna S. Moore opted for the 1830 date as the year of the boat's construction. Relying heavily on contemporary newspaper accounts, she published her findings and conclusions in *Inland Seas*, the journal of the Great Lakes Historical Society:

> The date of her building has been given as both 1827 and 1830. I have been unable to find any substantiating evidence for the earlier date. The Detroit papers of the period make no mention of her building. Steamboats were news in those days, and both the Detroit *Gazette* and Michigan *Herald* faithfully chronicle the appearance of each new steamboat and record their arrivals and

departures. It would be an unbelievable journalistic oversight if the building of the first one in Detroit had escaped local notice.

In the Detroit *Gazette*, September 3, 1829, however, there is this note:

"Steamboat on the strait – A small steam boat is now building in this city for the purpose of plying in the straits of Detroit and St. Clair, carrying passengers between this city and Ft. Gratiot, Monroe, Amherstburg, etc."

This is followed by a longer item in the *Gazette* for October 1, 1829:

> "We mentioned sometime since that a small steam boat was building by Captain Burtis to ply in the Strait between Detroit, Ft. Gratiot, Monroe, Amherstburg, etc. Since that time we have had an opportunity of examining the boat which appears, so far as we understand such matters, to be a very beautiful model.
>
> She will be launched about the 10th inst. and commence her first trip on or about the 15th. For parties of pleasure, for strangers who wish to view the straits, and for citizens living on their borders, this little steamboat will prove a valuable accommodation. Our citizens generally wish to the proprietor (Captain Burtis) a handsome remuneration for his enterprise, and we have no doubt he will get it. It will be precisely that kind of accommodation which has been wanted for many years.
>
> When our beaux wish to treat our belles to the thing that is really handsome, they will engage the steamboat for an excursion to Grosse Isle and Malden or to Lake St. Clair and Ft. Gratiot."

These two notices, together with the absence of any mention of the vessel in the papers for 1827 and 1828, would seem to rule out 1827 as the date of her building. There is no account of her launching (promised for October 10) nor of her first trip in the papers covering the rest of the year, and 1829 is never given as the date of her building, which indicates that she was not completed until 1830....

It has been said that in 1830 she began her career as a ferry boat on the Detroit River. This I believe to be the wrong date. Captain Burtis had advertised frequently when he began running his horse boat ferry. A steam ferry boat was a greater innovation and such an enterprising man would surely have announced such a novelty to the public, but no advertisements appear during 1830. The 'reduced fare' quoted in the advertisement for 1831 to the river ports would surely indicate a second season. She was built avowedly for the river run and it seems reasonable to assume that she spent her first season on that schedule. The papers for 1831 offer sufficient evidence that she was not in the ferry business that year. In the Detroit *Journal and Michigan Advertiser*, March 16, 1831, under the engaging headline 'Duckling' appears this notice:

"Steam Boat *Argo*. — This boat is now undergoing a thorough refit, and considerable improvements and will be ready in a few days. It is expected her speed will be considerably increased as her engine and boiler are undergoing material improvements. Her first trip will be up to the flats and islands of the St. Clair river with a party of gentlemen for the purpose of gunning. Considerable sport is anticipated as it is said the islands are swarming with ducks, geese, and swans."

These improvements consisted of increasing her width four feet and building a larger cabin. In the same paper, May 25, 1831, is the following advertisement:

"FARE REDUCED"
THE STEAM BOAT *ARGO*

Will sail the present season as follows:- Will leave Detroit every Tuesday at 6:00 AM for Ft. Gratiot and back Thursday so as to leave Detroit on Fridays at the same hour for Mt. Clemens, and back Saturdays, and to Malden and back on Sundays. Terms – to mouth St. Clair, 4s, to Wm. Brown's 6s, County Seat, 8s, Black River, $1.50, to Mt. Clemens, 6s, to Malden and back 6s, to Malden, 4s. For every meal of victuals, 2s.

JOHN BURTIS"[1]

Three things are apparent from Moore's article. One, while the ARGO had been in operation since 1830, it began to ferry passengers on a regular basis between Windsor and Detroit no earlier than 1832. Two, the season she spent on the St. Clair river took place in 1831. Three, when the ship became a full time ferry, its route was not limited to Windsor and Detroit; it also conducted business at other ports along the river.

In 1831 and 1832 two steamboats were introduced to the river trade. They were the GENERAL GRATIOT and the GENERAL BRADY. Being larger and faster than the ARGO, they were strong competition for the little boat. An opportunity for John Burtis to captain one of these newer and more powerful steamers came early in 1832, and he sought to place the ARGO in other hands. On 12 September 1832, an advertisement appeared in the Detroit *Journal*, which indicated that the boat was being refitted for a second time, and that it "would hereafter be employed as a ferry between the city of Detroit and the Beacon Ferry House, Sandwich".[2] The advertisement was signed "L. Davenport". This would have been Louis Davenport, a native of Detroit. An agreement between Burtis and Davenport stated that "John Burtis, being owner of one third of the ferry business from Detroit to the Canadian shore, as well as one third of the steam boat ARGO – leases to L. Davenport the one third part of the ARGO for one year for $275.00".[3] This arrangement lasted until 1836, the year the ARGO disappeared from the ferry scene.

The ARGO was a small craft of dubious design. It was only 42 feet long, 9 feet wide, $2\frac{1}{2}$ feet deep, and rated at 8 to 9 tons. This is how Friend Palmer described the steamer: "She was fashioned out of two immense trees or logs, hollowed out like canoes, and the two were joined together fore and aft, but were spread apart and decked over with a centre piece and had side wheels."[4] The cabin consisted of a light deck supported by upright stanchions and was enclosed on the sides with canvas. She had a 4 horsepower engine, and her boiler was "in proportion". It has been said that if there was the slightest wind the ARGO's engine would not run, and she would have to be laid up until the weather improved. Though the ARGO had steam power, a decided advantage over the oarsman's back or wind in a sail, the little vessel was not without its faults. "She was awfully cranky, this little ARGO," wrote Palmer, "and it required considerable vigilance on the part of her captain to keep her passengers from 'shooting around' and tipping her over."[5]

In his book, *Early Days In Detroit,* Palmer recounted an amusing incident concerning his uncle, U.S. Senator Thomas Palmer. It seems the senator was a man of ample proportions. One day he was aboard the ARGO, and the captain felt he had to keep an eye on his special guest. Every once in a while he would sing out, "For God's sake , Uncle Tom, keep in the middle of the boat or you will have us over." Or, he would yell, "Trim ship Uncle Tom." Eventually, "Trim ship Uncle Tom" became a byword during a trip across the river on the tiny steamer.

We are not sure what changes Davenport made to the ARGO, but he felt confident enough to place an advertisement in the Detroit *Journal,* 21 September 1832, announcing the boat's re-entry into the ferrying business. Some of the local residents, though, were not too sure it would stay afloat, regardless of the number and extent of the improvements. In reply, Davenport published a rather sarcastic notice in the *Courier*:

> Short Excursion – We would commend all those who delight in short excursions to the care of Capt. Davenport of the steamer ARGO who, for a trifling consideration, will see them safe on board, safe across the river, and safe on the soil of "His Britannic Majesty William the fourth". Some wag has been pleased to christen the ARGO the boat of "forty mouse power" but we can assure all who

take an interest in the little creature's welfare, that in every way she is seaworthy, that she can sturdily out-ride any storm that may come up or down the strait (provided it be accompanied by a gentle zephyr), that her accommodations are quite comfortable and that in short, she is the Multum in Parvo of our western steamers.[6]

One person who enjoyed relaxing on the deck of the ARGO was Mrs. Anna Jameson, the Irish author and art historian. She recorded her experiences in her classic work, *Winter Studies and Summer Rambles in Canada*:

> A pretty little steamer, gaily painted, with streamers flying, and shaded by an awning, is continually passing and repassing from shore to shore. I have sometimes sat in this ferry-boat for a couple of hours together, pleased to remain still, and enjoy, without exertion, the cool air, the sparkling, redundant waters, and green islands; – amused meantime by the variety and conversation of the passengers. English emigrants and French Canadians, brisk Americans, dark, sad-looking Indians, folded in their blankets, farmers, storekeepers, speculators in wheat, artisans, trim girls with black eyes and short petticoats, speaking a Norman patois, and bringing baskets of fruit to the Detroit market, and over-dressed, long-waisted damsels of the city, attended by their beaux, going to make merry on the opposite shore.[7]

In the years to follow, there would be many more ferry steamers, each having their own story to tell, but the ARGO remains unique for being the first steamer of them all.

CHAPTER III

THE EARLY STEAMERS
1836-1850

The initial years of steam driven ferries on the Detroit river was a time of rapid growth in the number of vessels commissioned specifically for the ferry trade and in the size and power of these new boats. The ARGO, despite its limitations, had firmly established steam power as the ultimate in efficiency, reliability, and speed. Within two or three years of her appearance, bigger and better steam vessels were added to the ferry fleet. These were the "steamers", independently owned and operated, which provided the earliest regular ferry service between Windsor and Detroit.

The first to arrive on the scene after the ARGO was a boat with the romantic sounding name LADY-OF-THE-LAKE. Not much was recorded about this vessel, except that she worked the waters during the summer of 1834. We know nothing

The use of steam to power boats revolutionized the ferry business and soon a number of new vessels appeared. The ARGO (II) shown here, was built by Dr. G.B. Russell in 1848.
    – WINDSOR STAR photo

else. In 1836, Louis Davenport introduced the UNITED, which was probably intended to replace the ARGO. Built by Captain Henry Jenking, the UNITED was 80 feet long and had a beam of 20 feet. She had a "high pressured engine which ripped and snorted and sounded like the last wail of a lost soul."[1] If the wind was coming in the right direction, there was no need for her to signal her departure, her engine could be heard clear across the water from the opposite shore. Her inaugural run took place on 13 July 1836. Having a burden of 71 tons, she operated between Lower Ferry Street dock[A] in Windsor and Griswold Street in Detroit, and charged 18 cents per passenger and $1.00 per horse and wagon.

In his memoirs of the battle of Windsor, 4 December 1838, Captain John D. Sullivan mentions the UNITED and its first and second engineers, Robert Motherwell and his son, and its commander, a Captain Clinton.[2] Coincidentally, both Captain Sullivan and a son of Captain Clinton, W.R. Clinton, were closely associated with the Detroit and Windsor Ferry Company, which will figure prominently in the later chapters of our story.[3] According to Sullivan, none of the ferries was used to transport the Patriots to the Canadian side for their attack on Windsor. However, two steamboats, the CHAMPLAIN and the THAMES, were involved in the conflict:

> The Rebels had succeeded in landing on the Moy dock, owned by Mr. W. G. Hall, above Windsor and below Walkerville at present. As all the steamers had been laid up, the Rebels took charge of the American steamboat "CHAMPLAIN", a small passenger steamer running on the south shore between Detroit and Buffalo. They put her in running order as soon as possible, and two companies were ordered on board by their commander, General Putman. On the night of the third of December, after some delay in getting their machinery to work, as it was supposed, satisfactory to the engineer and captain in the important voyage of capturing Windsor and Canada, they left the Detroit dock about three a.m., on the fourth of December, and ran up the river and landed the two com-panies on the ice near the Moy dock. The first company, which was the largest, was under the command of General Putman, and they started for Windsor. The second company started for Windsor a little later. The steamer "CHAMPLAIN" returned to Detroit as soon as all were landed.
>
> The first the people of Windsor knew of the attack was hearing the report of firing between four and five in the morning, before daybreak. Then the guard house was on fire and the Canadian steamboat "Thames," which was laid up at Van Allen's dock, opposite Peter McLaughlin's house, was set on fire and sunk.[4]

Having escaped destruction in 1838, the UNITED continued its work as a ferry until 1853, when she was converted into a lumber barge. In the end, after 43 years, she was destroyed in a collision near the St. Clair flats. One of the Motherwells was the engineer on board, and he was killed when the boiler exploded.

The docks at Upper and Lower Ferry Streets gradually formed a central location on the Windsor side of the Detroit river for the loading and unloading of the ferry boats, becoming as early as the mid-1830s a beehive of commercial activity. This is how the future Windsor was described in a story from the *Canadian Emigrant*, 21 February 1835:

> It is a pleasing duty to notice the improvements which have been made in a short time in the vicinity of the Ferry. But a few months since and the traveller could only discover the place by finding himself opposite the city of Detroit, and if he happened to be an Eastern Patriarch journeying with his flocks and herds, wives and little ones from the land of steady habits to the Canaan of Michigan, it were doubtful if he could procure lodging for the night. Now his pilgrimage draws to an

[A] In the text I will refer frequently to Lower and Upper Ferry Streets. These were two of the better known locations on the Windsor waterfront where the ferries docked. Lower Ferry Street is currently called Ferry Street. Upper Ferry Street is the short street running north from Riverside Drive, one half block east of Ouellette Avenue. It was subsequently called Brock Street and Station Street. Today it is Viale Udine.

The Baby House, built around 1811, still stands in downtown Windsor as a museum.
— Ontario Archives, Toronto, ref. S11209

The Windsor Castle Hotel was the scene of the meeting in 1836 where Windsor received its name.
— Windsor Star photo

end in a flourishing town, and his heart is cheered with the promise of good fare by the sight of good taverns and handsome accommodations.[5]

The same newspaper filed the following report on 13 September 1836: "The meeting for the purpose of naming the village at the ferry, in the 6th instant, resulted in its being called "Windsor."[6]

Closely connected to the ferry business and the growth of the village that now had its own official name were the various hotels and taverns along the riverside. We have already referred to St. Amour's hotel and to the Pig and Tinder Box tavern. By mid-century, the most famous hotel was definitely the Windsor Castle, located on the ferry wharf between two tailor shops:

WINDSOR CASTLE ALE AND BEER HOUSE

S.T. Provett respectfully informs the inhabitants and visitors of Windsor and Sandwich that he has opened a small establishment on the old country plan, where he always keeps on hand good schnapps in the Edinboro ale, Sandwich and Detroit beer brewed from the London recipe. Soda water, etc., etc. A good snack in the shape of spiced beef and tongue, boiled eggs, pickled fish and a crust of bread and cheese. Tarts, crackers, etc., always on hand. Moreover, a private room where an old countryman or others who prefer it may enjoy the river breeze over a jug of the best beer this country affords and their pipe of tobacco or first-rate cigar. The Windsor Castle stands on the Ferry wharf between the two tailor shops.[7]

The introduction of new ferries continued apace. In 1845, the MOHAWK, a former British revenue steamer constructed at Kingston in 1842, was converted to a ferry boat and placed under the command of Captain Tom Chilvers. Working as a ferry for only a brief period, she was lost on Lake Huron in 1868.

During the early 1840s, Sam Woodworth, the son of Ben Woodworth, of Detroit's thriving Steam Boat Hotel, owned and operated two ferries. Sam used them in conjunction with his father's business, ferrying passengers between the hotel and Windsor. A jolly and likable fellow, Sam was highly regarded by his many patrons. He would often accompany them on the boat back to Windsor. On one such trip, as soon as the boat had docked on the Canadian side, he went up on deck and stood by the stack to watch the people disembark. Just as he was waving a hearty goodbye to everyone on the wharf, the boiler burst, and the explosion blew Sam and the stack fifty feet in the air, killing him instantly and spreading fragments of man and metal over a horrified crowd. Sam Woodworth was mourned by large gatherings of people on both sides of the river.[8]

François Baby (1768-1852), Windsor's most prominent Roman Catholic and French Canadian, was another independent ferry operator. His home, which was taken over by the Americans in the war of 1812, is recorded on the 1835 map of Richmond. It was near Ferry Street, and is now the François Baby House: Windsor Community Museum on Pitt Street. Baby was granted a ferry lease dated 14 March 1843,[9] several years before the Legislative Assembly of Canada passed an Act regulating ferries and protecting the rights of the lessees of ferries.[10] He built the steamer ALLIANCE, and it sailed for several years with Captain Tom Chilvers as master. In April 1851, Chilvers leased the steamer from Baby, receiving from him the rights to Baby's franchise and the use of his dock. François Baby meanwhile remained as owner-operator, a more genteel aspect of the business and one in keeping with his social status as a gentleman. Near the end of the 1850s, after Baby's death, the ALLIANCE became the UNDINE, under Captain John Sloss. The change in name coincided with a major overhaul of the vessel. On 30 March 1859, the following appeared in the Detroit *Free Press*:

NEW STEAM FERRY

The steamer "UNDINE", having been thoroughly overhauled and refurnished will commence her regular trips from the foot of Woodward Avenue to Dougall's dock in Windsor on Wednesday morning March 30. The steamer

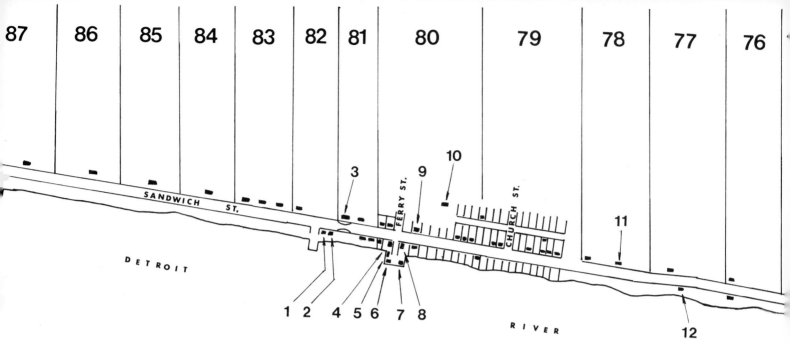

87 86 85 84 83 82 81 80 79 78 77 76

SANDWICH ST.

DETROIT

FERRY ST.

CHURCH ST.

3   9   10

1 2 4 5 6 7 8

11

12

RIVER

1. THE ST. AMOUR TAVERN AND FERRY.
2. ST. AMOUR'S WIDOW'S RESIDENCE.
3. MR. VITAL OUELLETTE'S RESIDENCE.
4. GROCERY AND PROVISIONS STORE OF
   MR. L. AND MR. H. DAVENPORT.
5. MR. ASK'S TAILOR SHOP.
6. MR. J. PERRY'S TAILOR SHOP.
7. THE FERRY.
8. THE J. AND J. DOUGALL STORE, WAREHOUSE AND WHARF.
9. MR. JAMES DOUGALL'S RESIDENCE.
10. MR. BABY'S RESIDENCE.
11. MR. JANETTE'S RESIDENCE.
12. THE PIG AND TINDER BOX TAVERN AND FERRY,
    LABALAINE'S OLD STAND, NOW RUN BY MR. MCLEAN.

WINDSOR IN 1835 (RICHMOND)

Redrawn by the author from an original by
Geo. F. Macdonald 1921

will make regular trips from 6 a.m. to 9.p.m. (Sundays included) when a small boat will be put on to accommodate those who wish to cross at a late hour. By careful management and politeness of the officers of the boat, it is hoped a liberal patronage will be secured.[11]

By the middle of the nineteenth century, the ferry business between Windsor and Detroit was very competitive

and thriving. One indication of its importance was the erection of a custom house as early as 1841. Windsor officially became a port of entry on 27 December 1854.[12]

Dr. George B. Russell, of Detroit, who was Louis Davenport's son-in-law, was the next important player to enter the ferry sweepstakes. In 1848, he launched the ARGO II. It was 100 feet in length, with a beam of 20 feet, making it the longest ferry on the river. Another first was the introduction of enclosed cabins on both sides of the deck. However, the ARGO II began its existence on a tragic note. After only a very brief run, its boiler exploded. The captain, first mate, and a few others were killed. Dr. Russell was not to be deterred. In short order, he had the steamer refitted and placed in service under the command of Captain W. C. Clinton and Captain James Forbes. Under these two men, the ARGO II worked steadily without another mishap on her record. She retired in 1872.

During this period, the steam ferries offered a new form of entertainment for the local residents. For the price of one round trip ticket, passengers were allowed to ride back and forth across the river as often as they wished so long as they did not get off the boat. It was an offer few people could resist. On warm spring days and hot summer nights, the ferries were often crammed to overflowing. George W. Osborn was one of those who loved to ride the ferries this way, and he recorded his feelings in a poem:

RIDING ON THE FERRY

When the mercury denotes
Sultry summer heat,
Then the spacious ferry boats
Afford a cool retreat.
On a shady upper deck,
Joined by friends so merry,
Bless me! ain't it pleasant,
Riding on the ferry?

Back and forth from shore to shore,
On the rippling river,
Watching spray beads rise and fall,
Where the sunbeams quiver;
Revelling in the cooling breeze,
Every one is cheery;
Bless me! ain't it pleasant
Riding on the ferry?

Now your sitting vis-a-vis
With a charming creature,
Happiness is in her eye,
Joy in every feature.
"Isn't this superb?" she asks,
"Yes" you answer, "very"
Bless me! ain't it pleasant,
Riding on the ferry.

Thus the heated hours are passed-
Laughing, joking, singing;
Joyous shouts from happy groups
On the cool breeze ringing.
Now you see your charmer home,
Feeling blithe and merry,
Cause engaged to go to-morrow
Riding on the ferry. [13]

Friend Palmer also thought highly of the idea:

Another pleasing feature about this ferry business is the liberality of the company in allowing the public to enjoy in season the luxury of riding on their boats from morning until evening for 10 cents each person; children in baby carriages and arms free. Just think of it! Nowhere else in the world can this be duplicated, nor the routes either, for that matter. In the early days no such luxury was dreamed of. It was available to a limited extent, but no one ever thought of taking advantage of it. [14]

The ferries were also known as the "10 cent babysitter". It was a common practice for many mothers, who wanted a few hours of freedom to shop, to place their children on board one of the ferries and leave instructions for them to watch for her on the dock at the end of each trip. Once she was finished her shopping, she would be there to wave them off the boat. It seems that the ferry owners would do anything for a dime, and that people were very trusting of the captains and their mates to keep an eye open for their little ones.

Nothing lasts forever. The all day fares and the "10 cent babysitters" came to an end. Profits had plunged, and profits were everything to the individuals who owned the ferries.

The UNION, when she was launched in 1857, became the principal railway ferry in the Windsor-Detroit area.
– THE MORRISON LITERARY PAPERS, MUNICIPAL ARCHIVES, WINDSOR PUBLIC LIBRARY.
REPRODUCED COURTESY OF THE ESSEX COUNTY HISTORICAL SOCIETY

CHAPTER IV

THE RAILWAY FERRIES

It was Tuesday, 17 January 1854. The crowds had been gathering all day long at the newly erected railway station at the foot of Upper Ferry Street. They were anxiously waiting and watching for the arrival of the first steam locomotive in Windsor on the recently completed Great Western Railway. The GWR linked Toronto and Niagara and New York State with Windsor and Detroit and the American mid-west. The story of the ferries would be incomplete without considering the part the railway played in the development of transportation on the Detroit river.

Before the railway came to Windsor, the tiny settlement was reached either by the Great Lakes or by a primitive stage route that went as far as Toronto and Niagara. Of course, the winter months — the ice in particular — severely curtailed water travel. In the summer, sudden and violent storms on the lakes were the greatest danger. The nineteenth century witnessed a litany of sunken ships. The alternative, though, could be an extremely unpleasant experience for even the hardiest traveller. The stage coach ride was bone-jarring any time of the year and horribly cold in the winter.

For the American, going from Chicago and other points west to New York State and the eastern seaboard, the trip around Lake Erie was a long and tiring trek. However, the distance between Detroit and Buffalo, by way of Canada, was significantly shorter. In due time, then, many Americans took advantage of this by crossing at Detroit and picking up a stage in Windsor. This provided extra income for the local stage operators. To promote their business, they advertised in the local papers:

> Stages will leave Windsor every morning at 9 o'clock during the close of navigation, for Buffalo and intermediate points. Fare to Buffalo $14.00 including ferriage. Through in three days.[1]

This cosy relationship quickly fell victim to the GWR.

The railway brought prosperity and romance to Windsor over the years, and it also brought thousands of travellers and countless tons of freight. Most of the passenger and freight traffic was bound for points in the United States, and this required a trip across the river. The GWR had built their line to the Canadian gauge of 5'6", making it impossible for its rolling stock to be used on the U.S. system and vice-versa. To continue the journey, then, both passengers and freight had to be unloaded in Windsor, ferried across, and reloaded on the American trains.

Initially, the local ferries provided this service from a new ferry dock built at the foot of Upper Ferry Street near the railway station. This arrangement was only temporary. Within weeks the GWR had purchased a ferry and put it in operation from a dock that it had built just east of the new station. The TRANSIT was a side-wheeled bulk steamer, which connected the GWR with the Michigan Central Railway at its Third Street dock in Detroit. A second railway steamer, the NIAGARA, was purchased at the same time as the TRANSIT, but little information is available on this ship.

The TRANSIT was soon followed by the OTTAWA. Dr. Geo. B. Russell had built this boat in 1852 for the ferry trade, and in 1854 he leased it to the Detroit & Milwaukee Railroad to run between the Great Western depot in Windsor and their Brush Street dock in Detroit. In 1856, Dr. Russell built yet another ferry, the 250 ton side-wheeled bulk steamer WINDSOR. Soon after entering service on the Detroit river, she too was leased to the railways for the Great Western and Detroit and Milwaukee run. The OTTAWA and the WINDSOR worked together on the railway ferry route, the OTTAWA carrying freight and the WINDSOR carrying passengers and freight.

The WINDSOR played an important role in the development of the area when, on 16 July 1857, she laid the first submarine telegraph lines under the Detroit river. The line was laid from east Detroit to Belle Isle, across the island, and then from the island to the Canadian shore. The following day the submarine cable was attached to the telegraph cables of both communities, and messages were immediately received in Detroit from as far away as Toronto and Montreal.

In 1860, the Prince of Wales, who later became King Edward VII, made a tour of Canada landing at St. John's Newfoundland on 23 July 1860. Two months later, on September 20th, his tour brought him to Windsor. N.F. Morrison, in his Radio Sketches of 20 June 1959, describes his visit to Windsor:

The loyal little town of Windsor (population about 2,500) was gaily decorated and alive with excitement. Mayor James Dougall had proclaimed Thursday, September 20, 1860 as a public holiday but during the morning torrents of rain descended. At noon, however, the clouds broke away and the sun shone forth pleasantly. At 3 o'clock a company of light artillery, invited by the civic authorities, arrived from London to fire a salute in honour of the Prince when he reached Windsor. They marched to the public square beside the town hall (now a storage building at 255 Riverside Drive East), and there they deposited their artillery for use in the evening. The royal train arrived at the station punctually at 8 o'clock and was received with cheers from the large crowd that had collected, the firing of cannon, display of fireworks, huge bonfires and general rejoicings by the whole people of Windsor, who had found it almost impossible to restrain their enthusiasm. The illuminations were set in a blaze and the town presented a most beautiful appearance.

As the royal party passed through the covered way that had been erected from the station to the steamer landing whence they would depart for Detroit, formal addresses were presented. After their very brief visit in Windsor, the royal party embarked on the beautifully-decorated steamer Windsor, where the governor of Michigan, mayor and aldermen of Detroit and other prominent citizens were waiting to receive them.

Subsequently the Prince and his suite proceeded to positions for observation on the forward deck of the Windsor, from which they beheld a line of steamers in the centre of the river "all beautifully illuminated with lamps of various colours". As the Windsor passed the first of these ships, a shower of rockets and candles were let off, a signal that was answered by the whole fleet, filling the river with illumination. From the deck of the steamer Windsor "the whole village of Windsor seemed as if in a blaze of light. Every house was illuminated, bonfires were blazing in all directions, and rockets filled the air. Fireworks were discharged from all the vessels in the stream, while many of the large warehouses and other buildings on the wharf at Detroit were brilliantly illuminated. The extensive wharves of the Detroit and Milwaukee and Michigan Central railways were also illuminated, adding very greatly to the general effect upon the river.

On approaching the landing at the foot of Woodward Avenue, the long line of torches borne by the firemen disclosed to view the immense crowd of people that thronged the spacious avenue from the intersection of Jefferson Avenue to the water's edge, from whom as the boat neared the dock, a shout of welcome went up that must have caused a thrill to go through the heart of the Prince.[2]

Many local citizens were quite critical of the Prince's brief stay in Windsor. Joe Jenking reflected these feelings in a 1902 interview:

The present King Edward crossed on my boat to Detroit when he visited in 1860. I was on board at the time, and I tell you the people of Windsor were huffed when the prince was hurried across the river without waiting to receive a welcome from his mother's subjects. I was pretty mad myself [3]

In 1856, the railways bought a ten-year old screw-driven ferry called the GLOBE. It was used to ferry cattle across the river, but her time was short. On 9 March 1858, due to a

The GREAT WESTERN was the first ferry built to carry railway cars and passengers across the river and the accommodations included a fine dining room.

– Windsor Star photo

The original Great Western railway station was built next to the river just east of Upper Ferry street. In this picture the old station has been converted to freight sheds.
— NATIONAL ARCHIVES OF CANADA, REF
PA30532

This is the type of locomotive which steamed into Windsor on 17 January, 1854, opening a new line from Toronto and Niagara.
— WINDSOR STAR PHOTO

rush of cattle on board, she capsized and sank at the Detroit Third Street dock. All of the cattle swam ashore; some, though, swam across the river to the Canadian side.

In 1857, the GWR contracted shipbuilder Henry Jenking of Walkerville to build a powerful ferry to be named UNION. She was a large side-wheeled steamer with an iron-sheathed hull, double smoke stacks and a large cabin and dining-room on the upper deck. "She was be equipped with powerful condensing engines, consisting of two cylinders placed in the hold at an incline angle to connect direct with the wheel shaft."[4] Smaller ferries at that time burned wood for fuel, but the UNION was a coal burning boat, and a coaling dock was built at the foot of Church Street in Windsor. The UNION, when she was launched in June 1857, became the principal railway ferry on the Michigan Central Third Street dock run, replacing the TRANSIT. The TRANSIT, in turn, was given the unromantic function of ferrying cattle across the river, which she continued to do until 1867.

On the night of 26 April 1866, tragedy struck the railway ferries when the WINDSOR was accidentally set afire at the Brush Street dock in Detroit. The ferryboat had just tied up, and a gang of freight handlers was loading a railway car with twenty-five barrels of naphtha. Beside the freight train stood a passenger train waiting for additional passengers from the ferry. A barrel of naphtha was observed to be leaking badly, and an unidentified man started to examine it with a lighted lantern in hand. There was a violent explosion, which scattered blazing naphtha in all directions. The remaining naphtha in the railway car and on the dock caught fire immediately, and soon the freight and passenger trains, the dock, and the WINDSOR were wrapped in flames. Several dock hands jumped aboard the steamer as their only means of escape, but the lines holding her fast were ablaze and the steamer broke loose and started drifting down the river. The fire cut off all means of escape to the dock, and the ferry passengers were forced to jump into the cold dark waters of the Detroit river. Twenty-eight lives were reported lost by fire or drowning. The remaining passengers were rescued by locals in small boats. The captain of the steamer DETROIT described what happened that night:

You see it was this way. Long about eleven o'clock one night an explosion of oil occurred aboard the steamer WINDSOR, while she was tied to her wharf at the foot of Brush Street. I was captain of the old city ferry, the DETROIT, at the time, and we had just landed at the foot of Woodward Avenue, with passengers from Windsor. I was standing at the signal ropes on the bridge leading to the pilot house when the WINDSOR took fire. In less than two minutes after the explosion she was a mass of flames from stem to stern. She had perhaps fifty people aboard as I found out afterwards – passengers and deck hands. In about another minute I saw her lines ablazin'-saw 'em part and saw the WINDSOR startin' to drift down in our direction. By this time the freight sheds on the wharf had caught fire, and I saw men and women leaping over the WINDSOR's rail into the water. I signalled our boys to man the life-boats, and shouted to 'em to make a line fast to her stern. This they did in short order. Then I sends a signal below to back her hard – runs into the pilot house, throws over the helm, and out and away we goes toward the middle grounds. I saw the men in our life-boats trying to rescue those people in the river- and they were surely doing their best. All at once, like the report of a gun, our two line parted. The WINDSOR was a roaring furnace. We were then off the foot of Wayne Street, on the middle ground where the cross-current runs strong, and I knew unless we could do something to keep the WINDSOR off shore, then when she struck, the whole river-front would soon be ablaze, in consequence of her drifting down with the current. But how to keep her out in the channel was sure enough a puzzler. First I decided to ram her down the river. No, this plan wouldn't do. The DETROIT would catch fire and then – what of my passengers – more than a score of 'em. On the other hand, the WINDSOR was drifting fast toward shore. We would have to ram her-and quick.

My men being out in the lifeboats left us short-handed – only myself, the wheelsman, engineer, and fireman, and the latter two would have to stay below. Lifeboats or no lifeboats, we must run the risk. I gave orders to send her full speed ahead – shouted to the passengers and the men to wet down the decks and stand ready with the buckets. Well, in a couple of minutes we struck her. There was a crash of fallin', blazin' timbers. The sparks fell on our decks in a shower and we were ablaze in a dozen places. But we held on to the WINDSOR, stuck to her, pushed her out into the river, fought the flames on board our boat and headed for Sandwich Point. All told we must have been two hours gettin' her beached, where she burned to the water's edge.

Next day a dozen or so Detroit citizens came aboard and offered me a purse of one thousand dollars in gold. Said I had to take it – that I saved the river-front. I refused and laughed 'em out of the notion. Why, anybody who was half a man would have done his best that night of the fire.[5]

Following the fire, the WINDSOR was rebuilt as a barge and served for many more years on the river, but never again as a ferry. The WINDSOR was not the only railway ferry to burn. After she was taken off the ferry route, the UNION was laid up at Sarnia on the St. Clair river, where she too burned to the water's edge.

The Canadian railways soon recognized the error of building to an off-standard gauge, and in the mid 1860's they began to lay a third rail along its right of way. This would permit interchangeability with American rolling stock. To complete the transition, the GWR placed a contract for its first railway car ferry. Called, quite naturally, the GREAT WESTERN, she was known locally as the "iron boat" since she was the first vessel in this area to have a hull constructed entirely of iron. She initially had a full length enclosure built over her tracks which made her resemble a floating tube. The company realized, however, that the "tube" turned into a wind tunnel in strong winds, and made steering the vessel difficult. For this reason and because of weight considerations, most of the tube was eventually removed. The iron hull was built on the Clyde in Scotland by the Barclay Curle Company of Glasgow, and shipped in 10,878 separate pieces to the shipbuilding firm of Henry Jenking in Walkerville for assembly. The engine was built at Dundas, Ontario and the boilers by the GWR shops in Hamilton.[6] Her launching on 6 September 1866 inaugurated a new method of transporting railway passengers and freight at Windsor and Detroit, both being ferried across the river in their original cars. This eliminated the need for a separate ferry boat, and another era passed into history.

The railway ferry system continued to grow. New steamers were added as business expanded. The twin-screw ferry TRANSIT II and the large side-wheeled ferry MICHIGAN were built at the Jenking shipyard, in 1872 and 1873 respectively, and added to the Great Western fleet. After the GWR was absorbed by the Grand Trunk Railway of Canada, in August 1882, the steamers HURON and LANSDOWNE (1875 and 1891 respectively) were added to the Windsor-Detroit service. These two ferries have also passed into history, but the LANSDOWNE is now a floating restaurant on the American side of the river.

In 1882, the GWR merged with its arch rival, the Grand Trunk Railway. In January 1923 the GTR was absorbed by the Canadian National Railway. The CNR continued to operate the railway ferries at Windsor and Detroit, but discontinued the ferrying of passengers in September 1955. Those passengers continuing their journey by railway were bussed to the opposite shore through the Detroit and Windsor Tunnel. Freight continued to be ferried across until 30 September 1990, when the barge ROANOKE propelled by the tug MANCO made its final trip. Today CNR freight is moved across the river on the Norfolk and Southern Railway barges WINDSOR and MANITOWOC.[A]

[A] Much more could be written about the railway car ferries of Windsor and Detroit, but this has already been accomplished in a excellent book *The Great Lakes Car Ferries* by George W. Hilton. This chapter provides only a framework of the part played by the railways in the early days of ferrying, and it is left to subsequent chapters to relate how this system affected the lives of Windsor and Detroit patrons in their quest for ferry service.

The LANSDOWNE, seen here sliding into her Windsor berth, (about 1935) is now permanently docked at Detroit, a floating restaurant.

The railway ferry HURON and the Detroit skyline taken about 1935.

The ferry GEM, built for
William P. Campbell, began its service in 1856.
– HURONIA MUSEUM, MIDLAND ONTARIO
J. SQUIRREL COLLECTION

The Jenking brothers entered the ferry trade in 1859 with the ESSEX. The two gentlemen sitting
in the buggy on the main deck are said to be Hiram Walker and son E. C. Walker.
– WINDSOR STAR PHOTO

CHAPTER V

THE SECOND STAGE
1851-1870

By 1856 the ferry service on the Detroit river had developed into a very competitive and sometimes profitable business. Four ferries were vying for patronage: the UNITED, the ALLIANCE, the ARGO II, and the MOHAWK, of which little is recorded. The captains of these vessels were constantly taking advantage of every trick and opportunity to increase their share of the business and to show a profit for their owners. Competition became even more keen when two new operators entered the fray. The GWR began ferrying in 1854, and William P. Campbell, an individual owner-operator, commenced his business in 1856.

William P. Campbell is better known as the father of Walter E. Campbell, who was to become the powerful head of the consolidated ferry company. In 1856, however, it was the elder Campbell who purchased a new ferry built by the Jenking Brothers of Walkerville, secured a licence, and entered into the ferry trade. This little steamer called the GEM was of side-wheeled design with both a closed and open deck for the "comfort of the passengers". The GEM was initially put into service between the town dock at Sandwich and Clark's Dry Dock on the American shore. The next year she worked on the Detroit-Windsor run where she continued until 1864, when she was replaced by the steamer DETROIT. The GEM returned as a night boat, but this lasted less than one season due to the boat's small size, age, and inability to generate a decent profit. In the end, the little steamer was purchased by Mr. A. Tregeant, who converted it to a screw-wheeled tug. Although the GEM disappeared from the river scene, Mr. Campbell did not. He remained active in the ferry business for many years, building and operating ferry boats.

During the 1850s, winter ice continued to be a problem, as it had been for many years, and ferry crossings were often unreliable. In the coldest part of winter, when the ice was two to three feet thick for weeks at a time, teams pulling sleds would be used for transportation. Tons of freight and many passengers were hauled across in this manner following a well defined trail. Individuals, too, could use this same trail to walk or skate across at all hours of the day or night in perfect safety. One enterprising young man constructed a frame shanty on the ice about midway between the foot of Lower Ferry street in Windsor and Woodward Avenue in Detroit, and put in a stock of "booze". He did a thriving business with the teamsters and their passengers, not having to pay a licence fee to any authority. This could be considered the first Duty Free shop on the Canadian-American border!

Although the steam ferries were far better equipped to handle the cold and ice than the canoes and rowboats of 100 years earlier, they still could not cope with the solid freeze-ups of mid-winter. With the coming of the heavier railway ferries, however, the river was kept open much longer into the season. Another factor which helped the ferries was the unique action of the river current at the foot of Glengarry Avenue in Windsor, extending across to the American side. Extremely fast, it would keep the river from freezing in this area for weeks after the rest of the river was frozen solid. Taking advantage of the open water, the ferries would dock at the railway pier at the foot of Glengarry and at a similar point on the U.S. side. But to reach the regular ferryboat landing or the town centre, ferry passengers would have to walk along the GWR tracks to Upper Ferry street. This could be a cold trek, but it kept the ferries running, and it was better than walking across the river ice. When heavy ice finally did stop the regular ferries in the dead of winter, the passengers sometimes sought passage on the railway ferries, as these boats could manage the ice longer into the season. The railway company did not normally accept passengers, but they were tolerated when the ice was heavy.

The DETROIT was built by William P. Campbell in 1864. Campbell was a staunch supporter of Ulysses S. Grant and Schuyler Colfax in the 1868 U.S. election and proudly carried their banner on the bow of his vessel.

– Author's sketch

In subsequent years, when the railway tunnel was completed, trains coming through the tunnel were sometimes used by those stranded on the U.S. side.

Winter did not provide daily commuters or casual travellers with a great deal of confidence in reaching their intended goal, but for most of them this was not a great concern. To have to spend a night's lodging on the "other side of the river" was an accepted part of travelling, and it could even provide one with an unscheduled night out at the theatre, a bar, or one of the local burlesque shows on Woodward Avenue near the docks. The ferries, though, did all in their power to keep running, to the credit of their owners and captains.

The Jenkings were well known brothers who maintained a prosperous shipyard on the Detroit river just east of the old town of Walkerville. Over the years they built many ships for the Great Lakes, including the large railroad ferry, GREAT WESTERN. In 1859, they expanded their business by building and operating their own ferry boat on the Windsor-Detroit run. This ferry was called the ESSEX, and her

captain was Capt. George Jenking who, the newspapers of the day stated, was "noted for the care and attention he gave to the matter of dress and to his personal appearance".[1] The boat had a surprisingly long career, first as a Windsor-Detroit ferry (until 1880), then for a number of years as part of the newly formed Walkerville-Detroit ferry system, and finally as a ferry between Sarnia and Port Huron. Her end came when she was destroyed by fire.

In 1859, Mr. W.P. Campbell, who had built the GEM, purchased a second steamer called the OLIVE BRANCH. This, if you recall, was the name of an early horse boat. Perhaps Mr. Campbell had a love of the past. The OLIVE BRANCH was intended for work on the Maumee river in Ohio, but Mr. Campbell purchased the vessel and put it into service (along with the GEM) between Windsor and Detroit. She sailed for a short time only, and nothing has been recorded of her disposition. In 1864, Mr. Campbell introduced another new steamer, the DETROIT. Built at Algonac, Michigan, it was scheduled to replace the smaller GEM on the regular ferry

The FAVORITE was built by Capt. John Horn initially as a night ferry, to accommodate Windsor citizens wishing to enjoy the attractions of Detroit after the regular ferry stopped running.

– Author's sketch

route. She had an uneventful career and was replaced in 1875 by the steamer FORTUNE. The DETROIT was then sent to the minors, so to speak, for she was put on the Sandwich-Detroit run, and ended her days in September 1885, the victim of a fire of unknown origin.

During the period 1864-1868, the active steamers on the river were ARGO II (G. Russell), ESSEX (Jenking Brothers), and the DETROIT (W. Campbell). The competition for fares between the three boat owners was intense, and though they fought continuously for daytime passengers, they could not be induced by means fair or foul to run their boats after six o'clock in the evening to accommodate late travellers. The regular fare for a trip across the river was 10 cents, and even the prospect of a 25 cent fare could not induce the captains to run a late boat. The exception to this was the GEM which was recalled into service as a night ferry for a short period. In his application to the Windsor Town Council for a licence, dated June 29th, 1866, Capt. J.R. Innes asked the council to "be as moderate as possible in the fee charged", as the night ferry business was not a very profitable one. Unfortunately, the GEM did not continue as a night ferry for very long. In the summer months late travellers could hire an oarsman to row them across, but in the colder months, they would be forced either to stay in Detroit or Windsor for the night or to cross on the railway ferry if one were available.

About this time, a number of prominent Windsor citizens, who occasionally wished to attend the opera, the theatre, or some social gathering in Detroit, banded together and approached a Capt. John Horn of Detroit. This influential group convinced Capt. Horn to put a night ferry into service, promising him their full and loyal support and a licence from the Windsor Town Council. The daytime ferry captains fully agreed to this plan for they thought that the night ferry would be unprofitable, and that the new captain would soon be forced out of business. They were to renege on this agreement, however, once they saw just how profitable a night run could be.

Relying upon the verbal assurance of the Windsor citizens, Capt. Horn purchased a partially completed screw-driven vessel from a Mr. Stager, who had run short of funds and was forced to abandon his project. Capt. Horn had the vessel fitted out as a ferry, and named it the FAVORITE. As a screw-driven boat, the FAVORITE stood alone in an era when side-wheelers were in vogue because they were presumably best equipped to break through the winter ice. But it was the FAVORITE which often came to the rescue of the side-wheelers.

The FAVORITE was launched in August 1868, and Captain William Cartright of Detroit was the first to command her. His first mate was W.L."Lew" Horn (who later sailed her as captain). In addition to acting as mate, Horn collected fares and threw the odd drunk on to the docks. The ferry ran from 6 p.m. until 12 midnight. However, if a party of Windsorites wished to remain later in Detroit, all that was necessary was to notify Captain Cartright, and a special trip could be arranged, often at a financial loss to the owner.

The steamer soon became a great favourite with the Windsor and Detroit people owing to "the genial manner and accommodating ways" of its captain. The night service proved an instant success and trade was constantly increasing. The day ferry captains quickly realized that handsome profits could be made. Despite their having promised not to interfere, they commenced running their boats late in the evening. By breaking this agreement, they angered Capt. Horn, who immediately began running his vessel as a day boat. To the credit of the Windsor and Detroit citizens, they continued to patronize the FAVORITE whenever possible, including the daytime runs.

Since the early days of the ARGO, the fare for a one-way crossing of the river had been 10 cents. No one had dared either to lower or to raise the tariff. This changed as soon as the FAVORITE began daytime runs. Battle lines were drawn, and they would have an impact on the fare structure in a way that would haunt the ferrymen for years to come. Captain Tom Chilver of the DETROIT fired the opening shot by placing a large flag on his ferry bearing the legend "Root Horn or Die". In retaliation, Capt. Lew Horn (now captain of the FAVORITE), placed a large banner on both the port and

The ferry ESSEX provided the title for this 19th century march composed by James E. Stewart.
Its picture framed the title page.

— FRANÇOIS BABY HOUSE: WINDSOR COMMUNITY MUSEUM

starboard sides of his vessel which read "No Monopoly —
Fare Three Cents — Ten tickets for a Quarter". This was
the first time a passenger could ride a ferry for less than 10
cents. What exactly was a reasonable fare was to become
one of the key issues between the "Ferry Company" and
the cities of Windsor and Detroit.

The captains of the ARGO, ESSEX, and DETROIT adopted all sorts of tactics to prevent the FAVORITE from landing
at the Brock Street dock in Windsor and at the Woodward
Avenue dock in Detroit. The FAVORITE was a small and
powerful boat, however, and Capt. Horn would work her nose
in between the stern of whichever ferry was at dockside and
the dock itself, and force the other vessel to let go or have
his lines parted. In this way, Capt. Horn normally got to the
dock when it was his turn.

The captains also pressured the Windsor Town Council to
pass a bylaw whereby a ferry which did not measure a sixty
foot keel would be refused a license. Capt. Horn promptly
placed the FAVORITE in drydock and measured its keel.
It was sixty-two and one-half feet. He immediately had
these figures painted on her bow in large letters.

In the winter, as soon as the ice appeared, the old side-
wheeled ferries were obliged, as usual, to "hunt for the
holes", while the FAVORITE kept running through the ice
for most of the season, much to the surprise of everyone.
In later years, she would prove her powers by rescuing the
HOPE, one of the most powerful side-wheelers. The secret
of the boat's success was her hull. Lew Horn put the
FAVORITE in drydock in the fall of its first year of operation
and sheathed her hull with iron plates. This gave the ferry
extra weight and a strong bow. A small screw-driven boat of
the FAVORITE's dimensions, cutting her way through four
to six inches of ice, upset all the calculations of naval archi-
tects and boat builders of the time. As a result, new designs
started to emerge from the drawing boards.

Becoming tired of bucking against the FAVORITE, whose
popularity had greatly increased with her ability to conquer
the ice, the other captains finally called a truce, allowing
her to run in the ferry trade unmolested for several years.

The ferry steamers picked up a little extra money by
towing sailing schooners from Detroit to Lake Erie, where
they could set sail safely. These schooners could not navigate
the river channels under sail, and had to be towed to open
water. On one occasion, while towing the schooner WILLIE
KELLER, the FAVORITE was involved in a serious accident.
Upon reaching the open water of Lake Erie, the WILLIE
KELLER set full sail and began to sail away, but the ferry
deckhand had forgotten to part the lines. The fast-moving
schooner soon pulled the line taut and rolled the FAVORITE
over, sinking her in twenty-seven feet of water. The cook, who
was in the kitchen between decks, could not escape and was
drowned. He was the only fatality. The steamer was quickly
raised. Refitted, she continued her career as a ferry until 1873.

Leading up to and during the American Civil war, thousands of slaves from the southern states escaped to Canada,
many of them crossing at Detroit by ferry as part of the
"underground railway". They were joined by many young
men, from both sides of the conflict, who had no desire to
fight. They were dissenters or draft dodgers. A full chapter
could be written about the various scenes that unfolded on
the decks of the ferry boats, as slaves, their owners, military
men, lawyers, and police (to maintain order) all boarded the
ferry boats bound for Canada. Careful scrutiny of the ferry
passengers continued for a time following the end of hostili-
ties in the United States as the draft dodgers sought to
return to their homeland. In time, these special checks by
the American authorities were relaxed and the public could
again enjoy a ride on the ferry.

The VICTORIA, built by G. Brady of Detroit and Capt. W. Clinton of Windsor, was named after Her Gracious Majesty Queen Victoria.

– François Baby House: Windsor Community Museum

CHAPTER VI

COMPETITION GROWS
1871-1873

The year was 1870. Although a tentative peace had been reached with the owner of the FAVORITE, a fare war continued to rage between the various ferry captains, and it became apparent to both captains and owners that larger and more functional steamers were required if they were to remain competitive in the ferry trade. But ferry boats were expensive, and it was not until 1870 that the next new steamer appeared. It was a large side-wheeled vessel called the HOPE, and it was financed by a local ferry captain, W.R. Clinton, and a newcomer to the ferry scene, George M. Brady of Detroit. In their application to the Windsor town council for a licence, the HOPE's dimensions were given as 104 feet overall length, 25 foot breadth, and depth of hold 8 feet, 2 inches. She had a one-cylinder, high pressure engine, placed in the hold just aft of centre, and inclined at an angle to connect directly with the wheel shaft. This engine had been taken from the old lake steamer UNITED EXPRESS, and it was said to be more powerful than any side-wheeler on the river at that time.

Capt. Clinton had always considered side-wheelers the most effective ice-cutting boat ever designed, and he assured the people of Windsor and Detroit that "no ice that came down the Detroit river would ever stop his vessel."[1] His boasting came to an end during the HOPE's first winter, when she was gripped and held fast by the ice. Clinton had to swallow his pride and ask Capt. Lew Horn of the steamer FAVORITE to come to his rescue. Horn came without a moment's hesitation, cutting a circular path through the ice around the HOPE, and even pushing the HOPE to shore. This incident and other similar experiences convinced Capt. Clinton and Brady that the screw-driven ferry was the better ice boat, and they immediately laid plans for the building of the VICTORIA.

In the interim, the two men put the HOPE in drydock and converted it to a screw-driven boat. This change improved the performance of the steamer, and she continued to sail until 1894 when she was replaced by the PLEASURE. The HOPE was then laid up near Sandwich on the Canadian shore, and, on 12 December 1895, it was sold to a Buffalo group for $5,000. The new owners, the International Ferry Co., used her as a ferry on the Niagara river.

As one can imagine, there were many amusing and dramatic stories told about events that took place aboard the ferries, as they cut their way back and forth across the river. There were stories of suicides, and of romance and heroism, and there were stories of murder too. One such murder story concerns a Mrs. Luke Phipps aboard the steamer HOPE. She and her husband were not on the best of terms, and Mrs. Phipps, it seems, could not resist the attention of other men. "If I catch you with another man, I'll kill you!" Luke Phipps was reported as saying to his wife in Detroit one day during the summer of 1883. Mrs. Phipps was indiscreet, however, nor did she believe that her husband would carry out his threat. She simply ignored him. Her end came the day she was persuaded by yet another smooth talking gentleman to take the ferry to Windsor. Boarding the ferry together, they were so absorbed in each other that they were unaware that Luke had come along for the ride. Luke watched jealously as the pair carried on their flirtation. The remaining passengers boarded and the lines were cast off. He waited until the steamer had reached Canadian waters and then walked forward. "I told you what I would do if you went out with another man again!" he is reported as saying. Then he fired three shots, instantly killing his unfaithful wife. Luke was arrested by the Windsor police, tried and sentenced to death. But he escaped from the Sandwich jail, and with two other prisoners he made his way to Detroit. Luke's freedom was short-lived, for drink loosened his tongue one night in a bar and he was re-arrested, returned to the Sandwich jail, and hung on 17 June 1894. The story did not end there. After the HOPE was laid up in the old Sandwich canal, the night watchmen reported seeing a ghost. They were convinced it was either Luke or his wife. A party of Detroit newspapermen went aboard the vessel one night to conduct their own investigation. They also saw a ghost rising from the mist surrounding the boat. After seeing it they went over to the spot where it originated and discovered two dead bodies lying there on the ground, their faces and hands ghostly white. Just as the frightened reporters decided to leave, one of the "corpses" got up and ran to a small boat. The "corpses" denied that they had planned the hoax, and stories about ghosts continued until police discovered that the old steamer was being used as a hide-out by a gang of smugglers. The "corpses" were later identified as two of the smugglers.

In 1870, W.P. Campbell decided to expand his ferry company. He purchased a steamer called the CLARA and placed her in service alongside the DETROIT. This vessel sailed for only the 1870-1871 season, under Capt. J.R. Innes, before being sold for service elsewhere. The CLARA's career was short and uneventful, but the boat's name is another in a long list of ferries to have worked the waters between Windsor and Detroit.

In a 1938 story in the Windsor *Daily Star,* Mrs. L.B. Tillson recalled that the initial sketches for the next new steamer were drawn on the dining room table of her grandfather's home in Windsor. This would have been the home of Capt. W.R. Clinton, and the table top sketches would have been for the steamer VICTORIA. The vessel, Mrs. Tillson said, "was named for Her Gracious Majesty Queen Victoria". Financed by Capt. Clinton and Geo. Brady of Detroit, and constructed in 1872 at the Detroit Drydock Company, the VICTORIA cost $9000. This was an expensive boat for the time, but the money spent to build it would not be enough to buy one of today's compact cars. She had a long sloping prow and could easily nose her way up on the thickest of ice floes, making her one of the best ice boats on the river in her day, and the

first to stay in operation 365 days of the year.

It was John Horn's turn next. In 1873, he built a side-wheeled vessel called ULYSSES S. GRANT at Sandusky, Ohio, and brought her to the Detroit River. She sailed as a ferry between 1873 and 1875, with Capt. Lew Horn as master.

By 1873, the rivalry between the ferry operators had reached the dangerous stage, the fight to secure the passenger traffic being waged incessantly. Things looked bad for all the owners, many of whom spent sleepless nights trying to dream up schemes that would divert traffic to their boats. It fell to the Horns to hit upon the most profitable scheme. German bands were a common sight in Detroit in those days. John Horn saw the possibilities of a wandering German band on board his steamer, so he hired a small group and placed them on the GRANT. That was a red-letter day for the passengers, who could not resist music, and for Horn, who reaped the benefits of an increased patronage. The band was so successful in attracting fares, the GRANT was paid for in three months. Meanwhile, the rival ferry owners were in a quandary as to how to regain their lost business. Owing to a shortage of docking facilities on both sides of the river, the boats would have to queue up and wait until the ferry ahead had departed. Once the passengers heard the strains of Horn's musicians, as he pulled into the ferry queue, nothing could entice them onto any other boat. Horn's competition was not to be outdone. The captains of the DETROIT and ESSEX also hired musicians, usually a harpist and a violinist. The captains of the HOPE and VICTORIA responded by introducing a new low fare of 5 cents. With his lead now neutralized, Horn had to look for a new twist, and he found it in the dance craze of the day, which was not unlike the dance crazes to follow in the jazz era of the 1920s and the jitterbug days of the 1940s. Mr. Horn cashed in on the craze by charging 10 cents for a ride and a dance across the river. This sent the other captains scurrying again, but it is not recorded if they too allowed dancing, or even if their boats could accommodate a "dance floor".

A funny incident took place one year on the 4th of July, a holiday, when many Americans visited Windsor and the

The HOPE after she had been converted to a screw-driven vessel.

– THE GREAT LAKES HISTORICAL SOCIETY, VERMILION OHIO

"playground" of Sandwich. Capt. Clinton and George Brady of the VICTORIA decided to hire the band of the Queen's Own Rifles of Toronto to ride their ferry for the day, playing for the large crowds they expected on board and at dockside. The band arrived at the Great Western station and proceeded to the foot of Brock Street to board the ferry. Lew Horn, who was always playing practical jokes on the other captains, heard about the plans and had his steamer GRANT at the Brock Street dock when the band arrived. The VICTORIA, as was often the case, had to pull in and tie up at the outside of the GRANT. To board the VICTORIA, the band would have to cross over the GRANT. This was not unusual. In a *Border Cities Star* interview, dated 20 October 1923, Mr. Geo. Horn (Capt. Horn's son) recalled that "you couldn't outdo the VICTORIA skipper though. He just laid his boat up on the outside of us and began marching his band back and forth from the VICTORIA to the dock across our boat, whooping "Hail Columbia" for fair, and pulling the crowd aboard his ship." Chuckling, Mr. Horn continued:

Then we scored again. Just to spite us once as the band passed over us, Captain Clinton told them to stop and play a tune on the GRANT. They just got nicely launched on 'Marching Through Georgia' when someone cut us free from the dock, and before the band could say boo, we were away and out past the VICTORIA, band, crowd fairly wedged on the deck and all. The band took it good naturedly and kept on playing while the VICTORIA came out and gave us chase. For two hours we romped up and down the river interspersing solos with band music, with the old VIC captain on the bridge shouting cuss words you could hear half a mile.[2, A]

All was not fun and games for the GRANT. Tragedy struck in 1875. A fire that started below deck spread very quickly and soon burned the vessel to the water line. The burned out hulk was towed to a dock in Sandwich owned by banker John Curry. There it sank to the bottom and found a resting place.

The approaches to the docks in the early 1870s were scenes of scurrying boats and harassed captains, vying against one another for favourable dockside positions and taking the odd risk to secure them. This was especially true on the Canadian side, where the railway docks were close at hand. One morning early in May 1897, the steamer VICTORIA was struck a glancing blow by the railway ferry GREAT WESTERN close to the Windsor dock. The VICTORIA suffered damage to her bulwarks both for and aft of the gangway, while the railway ferry, with her heavy bows, was scarcely scratched. The news account next day tells that "only one man was aboard the VICTORIA at the time, and he promptly took off his hat, coat, vest, and collar, and prepared to jump into the icy waters. A deck hand persuaded him to stay aboard however, as the ship would surely make dock, and the reassured man then made his toilet".[3]

[A] Some accounts give different details about this incident. Instead of the Queen's Own Rifles, it is the Fusiliers. The tune they played was "The Girl I Left Behind Me". And Captain Clinton caught up to the GRANT and regained the band near Sandwich Point in less than two hours.

Walter E. Campbell, who was to play such an important roll in the future ferry company,
purchased his first boat, the FORTUNE, in 1875.

– The Great Lakes Historical Society, Vermilion Ohio

CHAPTER VII

THE COMPANY

1874-1891

One can say that competition in the market place is good since it produces the best possible product for the least cost. This may be true, but it also must be said that unless the organization is making a profit it will be forced to close its doors. This was the position in which the individual ferry owners found themselves in 1872. The ferry trade had always been strictly a business, starting when the owners converted their ships to sail, then to horse boats, and finally to steam driven vessels, and continuing in the closing decades of the nineteenth century with larger, faster and more comfortable boats. But they were not enough. By 1872-1873, the owners realized that unless one of them obtained sole control of the ferry franchise for Windsor-Detroit, all of them might be forced into bankruptcy. A previous attempt to gain a monopoly of the ferry trade had failed. When W.P. Campbell introduced the steamer GEM, Dr. Russell owned the ferries ARGO II, OTTAWA, and WINDSOR. Fearing competition from the GEM, Russell chartered all the docks on the American side of the river, between the Michigan Central and Detroit and Milwaukee depots, except the city-owned dock at the foot of Woodward Ave. This is where the GEM docked, and she flew a banner advertising "One Cent Fare – No Monopoly". It was a brilliant move. The success of Campbell's campaign and Dr. Russell's high operating costs, broke the short-lived monopoly.

Circumstances were different in 1873 when steps were taken to gain control of the ferry business. The Province of Canada revised the legislation regarding the control and issuing of international ferry licences. An earlier law (1845) focused on individual ferry operators. The new law gave municipalities direct control over the ferry business.[1] Subsequently, the town of Windsor applied to the central government for the ferry franchise in its area. This was granted on 1 October 1863, for a period of twenty-five years.[A] The franchise gave Windsor absolute control of the ferries sailing from its shores, and the authority and right to grant licenses to ferry boat owners who could meet the franchise criteria.

George Brady made the first attempt to gain sole control of the ferry franchise by applying to the Windsor town council in February 1873. He asked for the "exclusive rights to the ferry franchise for the unexpired term of the government's lease to Windsor (15 years)."[2] Mr. Brady claimed that his screw-driven vessel VICTORIA had kept the ferry service open the previous winter. A special committee was appointed by the council to consider the application. After some deliberation, they decided not to grant his request.

The stage had been set, however, and soon other applications reached the council. On 13 October 1873, Brady and Capt. Clinton formed a new company under American Letters Patent called the "Detroit and Windsor Ferry Company". In May 1874, they applied to the Windsor Council for the ferry rights. Competing against Brady and Clinton were W.P. Campbell (DETROIT), W.L. Horn (ULYSSES S. GRANT), and Henry and Shadrack Jenking (ESSEX). Their company was the "Windsor and Detroit International Ferry Co.". They too made application to the town council. The ferry committee considered both requests, and both were turned down.

This action by the council forced the owners to continue operating as separate companies and to cope with the ever increasing competition and costs as best they could. But the methods used by the ferry captains to capture their share of the passenger trade were not always in the best interests of the travelling public. The active ferries in early 1874 were the HOPE, VICTORIA, DETROIT, ESSEX, and GRANT. Rivalry was carried to a point where a boat coming into shore would risk a collision in an attempt to crowd out

---

[A] See APPENDIX I for a copy of the ferry lease given to Windsor.

another ferry. At other times, the ferries would dock along side each other, two and three at a time, much to the inconvenience of the traveller who would have to cross one boat to reach another. In an attempt to ease the tension and reduce risks, the Windsor town council appointed a "ferry-boat starter". It was the responsibility of this man, John Forster, to order the sequence in which the boats would arrive at the dock, to time their stay, and to insure that each vessel left on schedule. His efforts apparently were not successful, for his position was cancelled.

Following these failed bids for the franchise, there was a lull in applications. During this pause two new steamers were added to the ferry route. In 1875, Walter E. Campbell, who was to play an important role in the ferry business in later years, joined the competition with his first steamer, the FORTUNE. This screw-wheeled boat had a 120 foot length, 42 foot breadth, and was of 200 tons. Her cost was reported to be $34,000 (the cost of ferry boats was going up), and she could normally accommodate 1,000 passengers and even up to 1,350 during peak hours. Campbell was the son of W.P. Campbell. The FORTUNE was built to replace his father's boat, the DETROIT, which was then taken to Sandwich and put on the run between there and Clark's dock on the American shore. She was on this route for one season, her end coming when she was destroyed by fire one night while lying at the Sandwich dock.

The second new ferry to make its appearance was the screw-wheeled steamer EXCELSIOR. Built in 1876 by John Horn, this boat would be the final link in design between the early ferries and the "modern" ferry so familiar to us all. Initially she had the square lines of a Mississippi riverboat, but after a number of years in service, it was rebuilt along the lines of a modern ferry. In her new dress, and renamed PONTIAC, she continued to ferry passengers for many years.

A Canadian customs officer was shot and killed aboard the EXCELSIOR on 25 July 1912. Officer H.G. Herbert had just arrived in Windsor from Ottawa that morning. He had refused a William Ferguson entry into Canada. According to the *Evening Record*, Ferguson was denied entry because "he was a cripple, having lost a leg, and was rejected for this and other reasons."[3] Ferguson was returned to Detroit on the next ferry, and Hebert, having business in Detroit, crossed on the same boat. No sooner had the EXCELSIOR left the Windsor dock than Ferguson fired 4 shots into the head of the customs agent on the deck of the crowded steamer. As soon as the passengers realized what was happening, they jumped upon Ferguson, and held him on the deck until the Detroit dock was reached. Attempts were made to extradite him back to Canada, but in the end he was jailed for life in the U.S. and died shortly after.

During the days of the EXCELSIOR a great hue and cry was heard from the public about the sanitary conditions of the boats. These ships were generally designed with two separate cabins on the main deck, one for the ladies and one for the gentlemen. The term "gentlemen" was questionable, though, because of the condition of the men's cabins and the behaviour of those who sailed or worked aboard the vessels. The boats were described in an article that appeared in the Detroit *Journal* of 5 November 1895. Under the headline "The Pig Sty Ferry Boats", the writer was unsparing in his criticism:

> The cabin of the EXCELSIOR is larger than a chicken-coop, but that of the VICTORIA is not. The latter is about 6 or 7 feet wide, twenty feet long, and about 9 feet high. At either end a few holes let in air. The men's cabin is a favourite haunt of the deck hands who find it a convenient place to light up their pipes filled with the vilest of tobacco, and expectorate at will upon the floor. They are also permitted to chew tobacco. The air is thick with ill-smelling smoke, and it is not fit for human habitation.

The writer goes on to say:

> We have spoken to a number of influential citizens of Windsor. They blame the prevalence of catarrh among young people on the fact that after they rush to catch a ferry on a cold morning, they are required to sit in a evil smelling cabin, and inhale the vile atmosphere.[4]

Some features of the EXCELSIOR resembled a Mississippi river boat.
   – Windsor Star photo

The EXCELSIOR was built in 1876 by John Horn of Detroit.
– FRANÇOIS BABY HOUSE:
WINDSOR COMMUNITY MUSEUM

After a few years in service the EXCELSIOR was rebuilt as shown above and renamed the PONTIAC.
– WINDSOR STAR PHOTO

I am amazed at the contrast between this, and an article written in 1878 by historian Friend Palmer. He states:

The present (1878) fleet of steamers consists of the VICTORIA, FORTUNE, and EXCELSIOR. These in point of superiority in their get-up and accommodations, are unsurpassed anywhere in the world. And what adds to this is that their officers are obliging and gentlemanly in their deportment, and spare no pains in caring for all who travel over this important thoroughfare.[5]

The Detroit *Journal* article had at least one positive result. Smoking in the cabins by the ship's crew was banned. Unfortunately, it would take many years before there were modern ferries equipped with spacious sitting rooms.

In the years after 1874, the various ferry owners continued to negotiate with each other in an attempt to resolve the franchise deadlock. Not until 1877 did they work out their differences and finally reach an agreement, banding together to establish a new ferry company called the "Detroit and Windsor Ferry Association". The ferry owners included in this new group were George Brady (HOPE and VICTORIA), W.E. Campbell (FORTUNE), and John Horn (EXCELSIOR). Mr.Jenking, the owner of the ESSEX joined the association in 1876, but he immediately withdrew his boat from active service. At a later date, the ESSEX was to play a major roll in the development of the Walkerville-Detroit ferry system.

Mr. Jenking's membership completed the united front the ferry owners needed if they were to succeed in securing the franchise. Their gamble paid off. In 1877 they applied to Windsor town council, and were awarded the much coveted franchise. For the first time in local history a single ferry group would enjoy the luxury of being the only carrier between the ports of Windsor and Detroit, thus ending the long struggle for survival by the individual ferry operators. The patrons could look forward to better ferry service, and the Association to higher profits.

One of the first steps taken by the new Association was to establish a central point for the collection of fares, in place of separate collections on each vessel. They approached town council, and, on 28 March 1878, council approved the erection of a collection booth with a gate.

Additional areas of improvement included schedules, sanitary conditions aboard the vessels, larger and more functional steamers, and dock facilities. Before too much could be accomplished, however, the assets of the new Association were sold to the Detroit Dry Dock Co. The sale had very little effect on the public, but it did herald the end of an important and colourful ferry era. Names such as Brady, Jenking and Horn faded into history, sharing the same fate as the vessels they had built and sailed over the years.

The new owners changed the name of the company to the "Detroit and Windsor Ferry Company", and placed Frederick Schulenberg in charge. Shortly thereafter they expanded this name to include "Belle Isle", calling the company the "Detroit, Belle Isle and Windsor Ferry Company". The city of Detroit had purchased Belle Isle and turned it into a playground for local citizens. The ferry company was awarded the tender for boat service to the island, and consequently they added Belle Isle to their name.

Another new steamer was added to the fleet. John Horn, who was one of the founding members of the original association, had drawn up plans for a new boat, and he had presented them to the Ferry Association in 1878. Launched in 1880 and called the GARLAND, it was a modern ferry boasting a new and rather exciting feature, electric lights. No longer would passengers have to grope around in the dim light of an oil lamp during a late crossing.

However, electric lights were the GARLAND's only up-to-date feature. In those days, cordwood was a source of fuel for the home fires, and as Windsor and the surrounding area had an ample supply, residents of the larger city of Detroit would purchase their cordwood here and return to Detroit by ferry. During the winter months, much of the wood would be gathered by horse drawn sleds, which made it necessary for the steamer deckhands to spread a liberal layer of snow on the decks to allow the sleds to ride smoothly.

Shortly after the GARLAND was launched, she met with an untimely accident while taking employees of the Detroit

A rare photo of Walter E. Campbell who despised the mere thought of publicity and would never allow his picture to be taken. Once, when one of the passengers aboard a Bois Blanc boat took his picture, he seized the camera and threw it overboard. Even here he tries to cover his face with an umbrella.

The GARLAND was the first ferry boat to provide the luxury of electric lights.

– WINDSOR STAR photo

BIRD'S EYE VIEW OF
WINDSOR,
ONTARIO.
1878

The town of Windsor (Richmond) and a very busy Detroit river in 1878. Some of the boats pictured are:

STEAM FERRIES	R. R. FERRIES	STEAMBOATS
1 *EXCELSIOR*	4 *GREAT WESTERN*	7 *NORTHWEST*
2 *FORTUNE*	5 *TRANSIT*	8 *QUEBEC*
3 *VICTORIA*	6 *MICHIGAN*	9 *HACHETT*
		10 *JAY COOKE*

–François Baby House: Windsor Community Museum

$40,000 IN GOLD.

Fourth Annual Free Excursion !

TO THE SUBSCRIBERS OF THE

Detroit Commercial Advertiser,

WEDNESDAY, JUNE 30.

ON BOARD THE STEAMERS' EXCELSIOR AND FORTUNE LASHED TOGETHER.

ON BOARD THE STEAMERS FORTUNE AND EXCELSIOR LASHED TOGETHER.

Twenty-third Annual Award of Premiums. Forty Thousand Dollars in Gold to be Awarded Subscribers. A BAND OF MUSIC ON BOARD. Subscribers must show their SUBSCRIPTION RECEIPTS at the Boat to secure admission. Subscriptions received by our designated agents and at the office of the paper, 44 Larned Street west, Detroit. SUBSCRIPTION PRICE $1 50 PER YEAR.

W. H. BURK, Publisher.

If you purchased a year's subscription to the Detroit Commercial Advertiser you were entitled to a free excursion trip aboard the EXCELSIOR or FORTUNE, said this advertisement.

– François Baby House: Windsor Community Museum

Stove Works on an excursion. Coming up the Detroit river near Wyandotte, Michigan, the steamer struck the yacht MAMIE, and sixteen persons drowned, eleven of whom were young boys. The incident received considerable local publicity, but it soon faded and the ferries continued in their trade.

The Detroit Dry Dock Company's plans for its newly acquired ferry business were short-lived. In 1883, the struggling company found itself with new management. This time a group headed by Capt. John Pridgeon purchased all the assets of the ferry company, including the rights to the lease, and immediately set about rebuilding the business. But the new owners ran into difficulties with the Windsor town council and the general public. The condition of the boats and docks, and the sailing schedule were called into question. Late in 1886, the town clerk wrote a letter to the company, informing them of their responsibilities:

Windsor December 14, 1886.

To the Managers and Directors of the Detroit, Belle Isle, and Windsor Ferry Company
    Windsor
Dear Sir,

I am directed by the town council to inform you that the said council last night had presented to it a very numerously signed petition, praying that your charter be declared forfeited on the ground that the time table established by the Ferry By-Law has not been observed by you, to the "annoyance, great loss of time, and serious inconvenience to the travelling public", and further to notify you, that you will be held to the strict observance of the provisions and requirements of the said By-Law, especially to the time fixed for the departure of your boats from the Windsor dock.

Believe Me Gentlemen
Your Obedient Servant
Stephen Lusted
Town Clerk[6]

There were other problems. The company was remiss in paying its annual franchise fee. The town clerk was instructed by the council to remind them of their obligations. Accordingly the following letter was sent to the company:

Windsor Sept. 18, 1886.

Manager Det. & Windsor Ferry Co.
    Windsor
Dear Sir,

I am directed to remind you that your ferry licence for the current year is not yet paid. Kindly have the matter attended to, and obliged.

Yours Respectfully
Stephen Lusted
Town Clerk[7]

The town clerk's letterbook, dated 1884-1889, contains many examples of such letters, indicating that this was not an isolated problem. The same book, though, illustrates that good feelings did exist between the town and the company:

Windsor Oct. 6, 1888.

Capt. Wm. Clinton
Manager D.W. & BI Ferry Co.
  Windsor

Dear Sir,

The town council at its last session passed the following resolution:-

"That the Council takes pleasure in conveying to Capt. Wm. Clinton, Manager of the Detroit, Windsor, and Belle Isle Ferry Company, their thanks for the assistance rendered by the said Company to the town of Windsor on the occasion of the late fire at the Water Works by bringing over the Detroit fire engine on the ferry Victoria and placing said boat at the service of said engine until the fire was extinguished, and that the Council donate to the D.W. & Belle Isle Ferry Company the sum of fifty dollars in application of such assistance."

In pursuance of said resolution I have the pleasure to enclose herein a warrant upon the town treasurer for the sum of $50.00.

Very Truly Yours
Stephen Lusted
Town Clerk[8]

As I read this letter in the town ledger, I wondered if Capt. Clinton laughed as I did when he realized that the town did not even know the company's proper name.

Capt. Pridgeon and his colleagues did what they could to improve the ferry service, but their efforts at reorganization were too little too late. In a surprise move the ferry company was sold for the third time, on 16 July 1891. On that day, Walter E. Campbell strode into the monthly meeting of the ferry company, held in their offices at the foot of Woodward Avenue, and with little ceremony he announced to the

Steven Lusted was the city clerk during the early years of the amalgamated ferry company. It was he who penned many of the letters sent to the company for payment of late taxes or for better service.
– ESSEX COUNTY
HISTORICAL SOCIETY

shareholders and employees that he and his associates had purchased controlling interest in the company.

Walter E. Campbell came from a family long associated with the ferry business. His father, W.P. Campbell, had built a number of Detroit river ferry boats in the earlier years. As for Walter, he had built the FORTUNE in 1875, and he was a member of the original 1877 Ferry Association. When the Association was purchased by the Detroit Dry Dock Co., he entered the lumber business. It was a move not unrelated to the ferries. Indeed Campbell's lumber enterprise would eventually re-establish his ties to the ferry trade as well as profoundly effect the future of the entire system. Pridgeon's eight hundred and eleven shares reportedly cost $110,000. Campbell's associates in the purchase of Pridgeon's majority ownership were his two brothers – Darius N. and Horace P. – George E. Avery, and S.S. Badcock. Under Campbell's direction, the company never looked back, and it remained in the hands of Campbell's managerial successors until the final boat ran in 1938.

This photograph of the Windsor ferry docks was taken around 1920.
– Courtesy Don Wilson, Windsor

CHAPTER VIII

THE FERRY DOCKS

Nineteen fifty will live forever in my memory. It was a good year, a year of beautiful sleek new cars, wide ties, malts at the HI-HO on Tecumseh Road, and late night stops at Heppenstall.[A] It was a year of swing bands and jitterbugging at a number of well known dance spots around Windsor and Detroit. Each one had its featured band and special atmosphere. One of my favourite dance spots was the "Showboat Ballroom" located in the Detroit & Windsor Ferry Company building on Sandwich Street at the foot of Ouellette Ave in Windsor. There, with a background of the Detroit River clearly reflecting the lights of the city beyond, one could dance to the sweet sounds of Claire Perrault's orchestra playing "Stardust". But the "Showboat" was not always a dance hall. It was once the centre of a very active ferry business, which carried hundreds of passengers and automobiles across the Detroit river daily. Nor was the ferry building always there, having been built long after the ferry business was firmly established in this area.

The story of the docks, like the story of the ferryboats, begins with the early oarsmen who ferried passengers in a rowboat. They did not have permanent docks. They simply pulled their canoe or rowboat onto shore at a place convenient to their fares, who would then jump ashore on the slippery clay and scramble up the bluff. The earliest ferry docks were the wooden wharves built by local oarsmen, such as Labalaine and St. Amour, on their own property. This type of dock was in use for many years. But, as time went on, more and more passengers were being picked up and put ashore at points near the centre of Windsor and Detroit rather than at wharves a mile or two away. It was this concentration of traffic that prompted the city of Detroit in 1806 to build what is considered the first public "ferry dock" on the Detroit River. It was located near the foot of Woodward Avenue. Although many other wharves would be built and used by individual owners, the Detroit dock would remain open for all.

One of the earliest docks on the Canadian shore was part of the Baby farm (later to become Lower Ferry street) directly across the river from "downtown" Detroit. It soon became the centre of the ferry trade in Windsor due to its prime location and James Dougall's excellent business instincts. Dougall was married to Susanne Baby, a member of the long-established and powerful Askin-Baby squirearchy of the border area. He was also an importer of British goods and had built a store and large wharf on the Baby farm. In 1831, he advertised in the Detroit *Journal*:

JAMES DOUGALL WHOLESALE IMPORTER OF BRITISH GOOD

Sandwich Ferry opposite to Detroit, begs leave to inform the American and Canadian merchants and the public, that he has received the principal parts of his splendid and extensive fall and winter supply of:

DRY GOODS, GROCERIES, HARDWARE ETC., ETC., ETC., FORWARDING AND COMMISSION

The subscriber has also built a wharf and commodious stores at the ferry, where he will be happy to attend to any forwarding or agency business that may be entrusted to his care.

JAMES DOUGALL

Before long other merchants joined Dougall, and the properties closest to dockside very quickly developed into

---

[A] Called Assumption Park today and located on the waterfront in west Windsor, Heppenstall was the name of a company in Detroit that advertised itself on a huge neon sign easily seen from the Windsor side of the river.

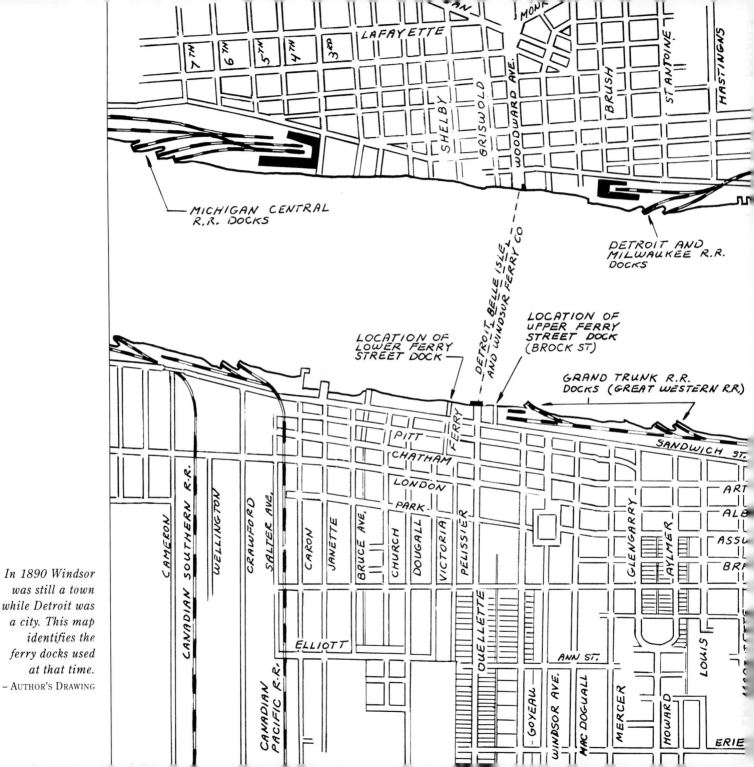

In 1890 Windsor was still a town while Detroit was a city. This map identifies the ferry docks used at that time.
– AUTHOR'S DRAWING

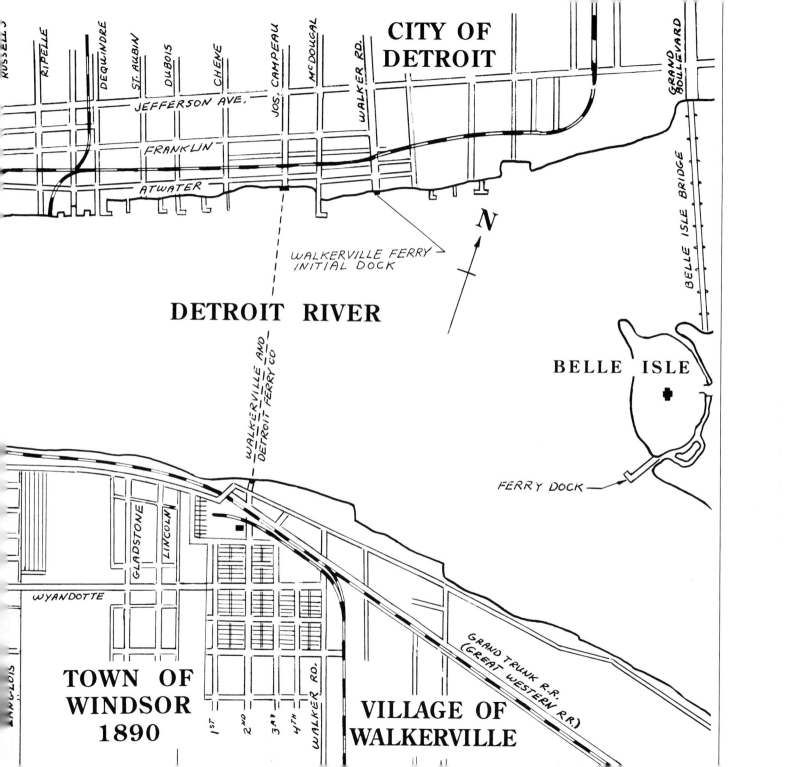

RUSSELL'S RIPELLE DEQUINDRE ST. AUBIN DUBOIS CHENE JOS. CAMPEAU McDOUGAL WALKER RD.

CITY OF DETROIT

JEFFERSON AVE.

FRANKLIN

ATWATER

GRAND BOULEVARD

BELLE ISLE BRIDGE

WALKERVILLE FERRY INITIAL DOCK

N

DETROIT RIVER

BELLE ISLE

WALKERVILLE AND DETROIT FERRY CO.

FERRY DOCK

WYANDOTTE

LANGLOIS GLADSTONE LINCOLN

1ST 2ND 3RD 4TH WALKER RD.

TOWN OF WINDSOR 1890

VILLAGE OF WALKERVILLE

GRAND TRUNK R.R. (GREAT WESTERN R.R.)

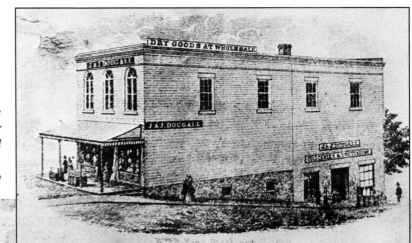

*James Dougall built this store and a large
wharf on the Baby farm. The wharf later
became the principal dock in Windsor and
was known as the Lower Ferry street dock.*
— WINDSOR STAR PHOTO

*Upper Ferry street and the Detroit skyline in the late 1850's.
The Upper Ferry House and people waiting for the ferry appear to the left.*
— N.F. MORRISON – GARDEN GATEWAY TO CANADA.
REPRODUCED COURTESY ESSEX COUNTY HISTORICAL SOCIETY

the commercial centre of the small village. Clothiers found this an especially lucrative location, selling not only to the local citizens, but also to visitors crossing on the boats. Public houses were opened in the vicinity to supply cool refreshment to the ferry patrons as they passed through. Edward Broadwell advertised "the best of ale, wines, liquors, and oysters etc. at all times" available at his "Upper Ferry House" in Windsor. Two other gentlemen, Fred Lauzon and Al Rivard, opened the "New Ferry Bar" on Ferry hill, dispensing temperance beers and soft drinks as well as light lunches. But all this was to change in 1854, when the Great Western Railway arrived in Windsor. With the railway came passengers and freight, and many of the passengers and most of the freight crossed the river on a ferryboat to continue their journey into the United States. The railway had built its terminus next to Upper Ferry Street east of Ouellette Avenue, some distance from the Lower Ferry Street dock. To accommodate this new source of ferry business, the town council decided in 1858 to build a dock at the foot of Upper Ferry street, next to the GWR station. This new dock was built on the site of the original Windsor "water works". The water works consisted of a town pump which drew water directly from the Detroit river. Anyone with a horse, a wagon, and a barrel could fill their barrel with "good clean river water" and sell the same in town for 15 cents. I wonder if a barrel of Detroit river water would bring 15 cents today? It was to this Upper Ferry Street dock that the town of Windsor sent the "ferryboat starter" mentioned previously.

When the dock at Upper Ferry Street (in 1938 called Brock Street)[B] was opened in 1858, the dock at Lower Ferry Street was abandoned.[c] This became a matter of great concern for the merchants on the west side of town. The new dock had taken away a good deal of their business. Over the years they attempted to carry on, but business continued to decline. Finally, on 14 February 1881, James Lambie, supported by other west side residents and merchants, petitioned the town council. They requested "that boats may be caused to run to both docks", and cited their losses as the

reason for their request.[1] The council in their wisdom agreed, and the ferries were ordered to run from both docks on alternate weeks.

This arrangement caused a great deal of confusion and inconvenience, for many times persons would go to one ferry landing only to find that the boat was running to the other landing during that week. This called for a remedy, and that remedy was brought about chiefly through the efforts of Francis Cleary, ex-Mayor of Windsor, and Dr. John Coventry, Mayor in 1882.[2] The town struck a committee, which included Cleary and Coventry, to resolve the problem. Their solution was to build a new dock at the foot of Ouellette Avenue which would be central to everyone. The land north of Sandwich Street (now Riverside Drive), between Brock Street and a point west of Ouellette Avenue, where the new dock would be built, was owned by a Mrs. Lucetta Medbury of Detroit. Cleary and Coventry approached Mrs. Medbury and succeeded in convincing her of the advantages to herself and to Windsor of opening Ouellette Avenue to the river. This agreement with Mrs. Medbury was confirmed in By-law No. 393, which was passed by the town council on the 20 November 1882. Work commenced immediately to clear the avenue to the river.

The first hurdle to overcome was a two-story brick building that stood exactly in the centre of the proposed extension. This was solved when a Chicago firm moved the building, without mishap, to a new location 150 feet west of where it stood. The right-of-way was now clear, and the town had the street filled in and graded to the river. Waiting rooms and a custom house were constructed. On 17 August 1883, the new dock was opened to traffic and free ferry rides were offered to the public. The Brock and Ferry Street

---

[B]   I will refer to Upper Ferry Street as Brock Street in my text from this point, and to lower Ferry Street as simply Ferry Street.

[c]   The Lower Ferry Street dock was reopened from 1875 to 1877, by Brady and Clinton, to be used by their steamers HOPE and VICTORIA. This left the Brock Street dock to the rival steamers FORTUNE and EXCELSIOR. When the owners amalgamated in 1877 all the ferries ran from the Brock Street dock.

Looking north on Ferry street to the Lower Ferry street docks about 1880. The vessel in dock is the FORTUNE.
— WINDSOR STAR PHOTO

docks were then closed but not torn down.

The agreement with Mrs. Medbury must have recognized her continuing ownership of the property on which the dock was built, for an item appeared in the *Evening Record*, 15 August 1893, which stated that the ferry company might move their boats back to the Ferry Street dock because of the high rent charged by the Medbury estate. The news caused an uproar among the Ouellette Avenue merchants, who would be adversely affected by any such move. Campbell denied the rumour in the very next issue of the *Evening Record*, and the matter ended here.

The Windsor ferry docks just prior to being torn down to make room for Dieppe Park. Note the Showboat Ballroom sign.
– WINDSOR STAR PHOTO

The Detroit and Windsor dock at the foot of Ouellette Avenue around 1890. The steamer EXCELSIOR awaits passengers. The small building on the left is the ferry ticket office, and on the right is the balcony of the British American Hotel.

— WINDSOR STAR PHOTO

CHAPTER IX

FARES AND FRANCHISES

1892-1908

On 1 October 1863, Queen Victoria, through the province of Canada, granted a ferry lease to the town of Windsor. The terms of the lease gave Windsor the authority to sub-let the rights to operate a ferry within the town's water limits to prospective ferry owners, and to collect an annual fee for these rights. The lease, issued for a term of 25 years, laid down certain conditions and requirements, but basically it gave Windsor a free hand in the ferry business. Four years later, in 1867, a new central government was formed at confederation, and it renewed the lease to Windsor for the remaining 21 years. Windsor used its authority wisely, granting ferry franchises to responsible boat owners, and collecting the annual fees. The town also used its authority to obtain the fairest rates for the passengers and to control to some degree the condition of the boats and the quality of service.

Around 1885, after the individual ferry owners had amalgamated and formed a new ferry company, an agreement was reached between the town and John Pridgeon, then president of the Detroit, Belle Isle and Windsor Ferry Company, The annual franchise rate was fixed at $300 per year. This arrangement continued until the fall of 1888, when the 21-year lease to the town expired. On 28 September 1888, a special meeting was called by the mayor of Windsor to discuss what action could be taken to convince the senior government to renew the ferry licence to the town rather than to any individual or private corporation. After a lengthy discussion, the council agreed that a memorial should be sent to the Governor-General-in-Council requesting that the lease to Windsor be renewed for another ten years.[A] This request was denied, however, and the control of the ferries reverted to the Department of Inland Revenue, in keeping with the new federal ruling that all ferries operating between Canada and a foreign country were under federal control.

When the new federal franchise was granted to the ferry company in 1888, by an Order-in-Council issued by the Department of Inland Revenue, the term was for ten years, and the annual fee was set at $400, payable to Ottawa. Within thirteen months this annual fee was reduced to $1.00 per year. No explanation was given for the change. In later years it was acknowledged that the reduction came as a result of a representation made by the company that "its expenses in connection with retaining the offices of the customs and maintaining all necessary conveniences in the shape of waiting-rooms etc. cost them a large sum."[1] In 1895, the year before a general election (when a change in government was expected), and three years prior to the expiry date of the existing franchise, a new lease was issued to the ferry company for a period of thirteen years, with an annual fee of $1.00.[B] The lease covered the whole of the city waterfront, and effectively gave the Detroit, Belle Isle, and Windsor Ferry Company a monopoly on the Windsor and Detroit ferry business.

The period known locally as the "Fares and Franchise era", the long and sometimes bitter dispute between the city of Windsor and the ferry company, began in 1892. The main issue at stake was the city's wish to have the best possible ferry service for its community, at the least possible cost to ferry patrons. Consequently, the fares charged by the ferry company became paramount.

Fares were certainly the central issue, but there were also other concerns such as dock facilities, and the condition and availability of the boats. Some aspects of the company's re-organization did not help matters. For example, in September 1897, Campbell ordered all company employees to live in Detroit. Even though the order was never enforced, the mere fact that it was issued at all irritated Windsorites so much that a group of them lobbied hard

---

[A]   See Appendix II for a copy of the memorial.

[B]   See Appendix III for a copy of the franchise.

to have the city take over the company, arguing that since three-quarters of the company's revenues originated in Windsor, it was only proper for the town to have its own ferry service. The argument was repeated many times as the town fathers and company officials became more frustrated with each other in their ongoing negotiations, but no serious action was ever taken.

As the era opened, the fare for passage across the river was 25 cents for ten one-way tickets. In the pioneer days of ferrying the oarsmen had charged 1 shilling, or 25 cents, for a one way trip across the river in their small boats, a fair compensation for the effort involved. Through the years competition among the ferry operators as well as government regulations reduced this rate to a flat 10 cents. This fare held until approximately 1870, when it was reduced to 5 cents by mutual agreement of the ferry operators. This fare was made obligatory by the Windsor town council in a bylaw of 15 June 1874. But there were several exceptions. In 1880, Captain John Horne of the FAVORITE reduced his fare to 3 cents, and Thomas Chilver of the MOHAWK actually slashed his fare to the absolute minimum of 1 cent.

Around 1879, the "official" ferry rate was reduced even further, this time by the new ferry company, which offered 10 loose or "strip" tickets for 25 cents. The company had hoped that the regular commuter would buy the strip tickets, and that any loss in revenue would be made up by the casual traveller who would pay the straight 5 cent fare. This did not work out as planned. Local residents also began using the strip tickets. Interestingly, the 25 cent cost of ten strip tickets became the standard on which the town would base all future negotiations with the company and the federal government.

In 1892, the year Windsor became a city, Campbell fired the first shot in the city-versus-company conflict, when he introduced a "monthly ticket book" that offered 100 rides for $1.50. The offer was aimed at the daily commuter. I am not sure why the book was called "monthly" since the 100 rides would limit its use. On the other hand, when one considers that most commuters worked six days a week (common at the turn of the century) and came home for lunch each day, 100 trips would last about a month. At any rate, "monthly" was the term generally used in contemporary news articles. At the same time the book was introduced, the company increased the regular fares, charging 25 cents for 8 tickets. Windsor commuters protested vigorously. Eight tickets for a quarter-dollar was too expensive. In addition, most of them could not afford the one time $1.50 outlay for the "book". Their protests prompted a stiffly-worded and sarcastic commentary from the Detroit *News*, 18 February 1892:

> Some ferry patrons living in Windsor object to the increased fares. Why do you live in Windsor anyhow? Why not spend your money where you earn it? Annex yourselves if the bleeding Dominion won't. You should only pay ferry fare once and that when you leave Windsor. If you must agitate on the fare question come on over and help His Worship, the mayor, in his demand for eight tickets for a quarter.[2]

The company relented. It re-issued ten loose tickets for 25 cents, and reduced to $1.00 the cost of a 100 trip monthly ticket book, which had to be used during working hours. The 100 trip monthly ticket for $1.50 could be used at any time of the day or night.

On 22 September 1897, the company moved to protect its profits by changing the ticket format. The company claimed that the "loose" tickets had a way of getting out of the collection box and back into the public's pockets. To stop this, they replaced the 10 loose tickets with a single card containing 10 numbers. This card became known as the "Meal Ticket". Each time the passenger boarded a ferry a company clerk would punch one of the numbers.

The *Evening Record* came to the defense of the people of Windsor, and published the following objections.

1. There would be a delay getting to the boats.
2. People in one family travelling together would require separate cards – more expense. [The *Evening Record* felt that each member of a family would be required to have their own card.]

3. Outlying people, who only cross two or three times a year, could lose their ticket and be forced into paying a straight 5 cents, to the financial benefit of the company.
4. A person could not purchase an occasional ticket from a friend.[3]

The third objection was rather week. Loose tickets could be lost just as easily as a card. Windsor's daily newspaper was expressing a widely felt hostility against the ferry company for having received a valuable franchise from the federal government for the ludicrous sum of one dollar a year. This resentment was echoed in the *Evening Record* of September 25th. The subject was the franchise fees paid by other companies: "Our own street railroad company, owned by Canadians, pays $500.00 per year, soon to be raised to $1,000.00, and the telephone company pays $250.00 per year. Why does this lucrative franchise, owned by Americans, pay only $1.00?"[4] The *Evening Record* of October 5th continued the battle cry: "the affairs of the ferry company should be in city hands and the franchise fees should be paid to the city's general fund. After all, the company does receive police and fire protection from the city along with most of its paying revenue."[5] Ottawa, however, controlled the franchise, and the city had to plead their case with the federal government. Late in 1897, city council sent a memorial to the Governor-General-in-Council at Ottawa outlining its concerns.[c] The controversy actually reached the House of Commons. On 31 March 1898, Ottawa told the ferry company to return to the loose (strip) tickets. This is how the *Evening Record* interpreted the events of 1898, in a story that ran eight years later:

> The latest imposition was the withdrawal a few years ago of the coupon ticket strip, in direct contravention of the contract, and the substitution therefore of what is known as the "meal" ticket, an innovation that has proved a source of serious public inconvenience and loss.
>
> A representative delegation of citizens waited on the minister at Ottawa about this meal ticket outrage, and their grievance was heard with apparent intelligence and patient interest, while the delegation were sent on their way rejoicing with the definite promise that the coupon

ticket would be restored. But the still small [Company] voice again got in its work. The department, apparently always predisposed to the side of the company, swallowed the plausible argument presented by the company's representative to the effect that the "meal" ticket was a literal and legal fulfilment of the agreement and the matter was dropped without any intimation of the fact being given to the city.[6]

And so the Meal Ticket continued.

In February 1901, the company instituted another round of fare changes. The use of the $1.50 monthly book was restricted to the hours of 6 a.m. to 9 a.m., 11.30 a.m. to 2 p.m., and 5 p.m. to 7 p.m. The $1.00 monthly book was cancelled. The company's intention was to provide cheap transportation for the people of Windsor and Walkerville who worked in Detroit, not for those taking pleasure or occasional trips. Again tempers flared. Windsorites, prompted and assisted by the local paper, pressed the issue with city council. At this time a new cry was heard over the cost of the trip to Bois Blanc (Bob-lo) island. It cost Canadian residents an extra 5 cents each way to ride to Bois Blanc, a Canadian island. Why was the company refusing to run its boats from Windsor, or to issue tickets that would take Canadians across the river and to Bois Blanc for the same price as the Americans paid for their trip? When approached by city representatives, Campbell's response to this issue was a flat "No".

One wonders how Campbell could have been so adamant in his refusal without fearing a backlash from Windsor City Council. The answer was given in the *Evening Record*, 5 August 1905: "It is not generally known, but the Ferry Company issues passbooks to the mayor and aldermen each year for use on all ferry lines including those to Belle Isle and Bois Blanc."[7] In the absence of conflict-of-interest rules that govern the behaviour of present day politicians, the mayor and aldermen took Campbell's generous gift, even though they were often called upon by the voters to lockhorns with the ferry company. Campbell's divide and conquer strategy was working. For instance, Ald. R.S.

---

c   See Appendix IV for details of this memorial.

Ernest S. Wigle was mayor of Windsor between 1905 and 1909 during the fares and franchise era.
– CITY OF WINDSOR

Foster pointed out that "there are two sides to every question", and then proceeded to present the company's position at a council meeting of 26 June 1906:

1. All but two of the company's employees live in Windsor.
2. The wages paid to these Canadians amounts to nearly $65,000.00 annually.
3. Sixteen of these employees pay income tax to Canada.
4. The company pays taxes to Windsor on $65,000.00 worth of docks and buildings.
5. The coal docks are located in Windsor, and besides the duty coming to Canada, Windsor longshoremen were engaged to handle the coal.[8]

The council was split over the issue. Foster's argument on behalf of the company was a reasonable one. Moreover, the service was good and fairly reliable. But the ferry committee, appointed earlier by the city, continued in its efforts to arrange suitable fare rates. On 26 June 1906, yet another meeting was arranged with Campbell and company representatives. It was held in Campbell's office. The committee received no satisfaction from the ferry company, according to the *Evening Record:*

"You go first, Mr. Mayor."

This remark is said to have been made to Mayor Wigle on the ferry boat, while the special committee were planning ways and means of approaching Capt. Walter Campbell, the president of the D,BI,& W. Ferry Co. Some such arrangements as follows might easily be imagined.

"No, Foster, you go first. You spoke on behalf of the company at the special meeting."

This Alphonse-and-Gaston conversation continued until the suggestion was made that Mr. Bartlet, being the best-looking man of the trio, should beard Campbell in the eyrie at the ferry dock.

Finally there was a compromise. Mr. Bartlet was to enter first, but Mayor Wigle was to do the talking, Ald. Foster to stand directly behind him in case he collapsed.

Here was the spectacle of Windsor's mayor, an alderman of the city, and a representative business man seeking favours on behalf of the municipality-an outraged municipality- from the head of the company controlling the ferry monopoly between Windsor and Detroit.

The ferry porter presented Mayor Wigle's greetings to President Campbell.

"Step in, gentlemen."

The soft answer turned away all wrath. It was apparent President Campbell was in good humour.[D]

"What can I do for such a fine lot of men?" suavely enquired Capt. Campbell.

"Er-er, ah, ah-we came to see if you could give us a little better rate on the ferries", spoke up Mayor Wigle,

---

[D] See Appendix V for a pen picture of Campbell.

who looked like a man who had just emerged from a Turkish bath, so profuse was his perspiration and so meek was his spirit.

"WHAT, HOW DARE YOU ASK SUCH A QUESTION?"

"Beg your pardon, captain, but the council sent us over. It is not really our fault—"

Ald. Foster felt the mayor's pulse, but the training His Worship had received in taming Ald. Trumble stood him in good stead for this ordeal. In a few moments Ernest was himself again.

"Well, I might as well tell you that the company cannot enter into any negotiations with the city. We are dealing with the Dominion government. Sorry, gentlemen, we cannot oblige you."

Thus spoke Capt. Campbell, and all the courage manifested by the trio in storming the presidio was wasted. All hopes of securing a "free-will offering" from the company were dashed to the ground and air castles were dissolved in the misty vapour arising from the river over which the ferries of the company speed with government-granted right.

After returning from the conference Mayor Wigle stated that the committee would go to Ottawa when the ferry matter comes up and an effort will be made to secure an audience with Sir Wilfred Laurier.

"I might add that the city need not expect any voluntary favours from the Ferry company," stated His Worship. "Capt. Campbell not only gave us no satisfaction but said the company would continue to operate its lines whether the franchise is renewed or not.

LEFT TODAY

The committee received a message to go to Ottawa at once and left Wednesday afternoon on the CPR for the Capital.[9]

The ferry committee may have buckled under Campbell, but the ferry riders still had a few defenders. The first of these was Archibald McNee, who came to Windsor in 1888 to assume control of the local paper. Shortly after his arrival, he turned the *Evening Record* into a daily, the forerunner of the present Windsor *Star*. McNee was a man of strong convictions. He did not hesitate to use his newspaper as a vehicle for his views on a wide variety of topics. His outspoken editorials and articles, and his unyielding advocacy of a municipal ferry service, raised the hackles of the ferry company. McNee was elected to town council in 1907, and he

Newspaper publisher and Windsor councilman Arch McNee campaigned for better ferry boat fares.

– F. Neal – The Township of Sandwich, Past and Present. Reproduced courtesy Essex County Historical Society

was one of the negotiators for the town in its dealings with Campbell. However, his voice on council and in committee was not as effective as his journalism. McNee was also a member of the public school board and of the Bruce Avenue Baptist church, where he was a life-long deacon.

The Hon. R.F. Sutherland was another defender of the ferry patrons. First elected a member of the House of Commons in 1900, for the riding of North Essex, he was very popular with the voting public and his parliamentary peers in Ottawa. Shortly after being re-elected for a second term in 1904, Sutherland was appointed Speaker of the House. He used his influence at the department of Inland Revenue to plead Windsor's case. On 23 June 1906, Sutherland advised the city that the ferry company had applied for a renewal of the franchise. This was his way of telling the city to make their move if it wanted any changes incorporated in the new agreement. "With Hon. R.F. Sutherland watching affairs at Ottawa on behalf of Windsor", wrote the *Evening Record*, 26 June 1906, "the ferry company will not slip a renewal of their franchise through the Dominion government before the city is heard from".[10] Mr. Sutherland's efforts to secure a square deal stirred the city to action, but this "action" was yet another committee, this time consisting of Mayor Wigle, Ald. Foster, and George Bartlet, to look into the affairs of the ferry system.

Meanwhile, McNee continued his battle for fairer rates, and on 5 October 1906, he wrote:

> These detachable tickets were found very convenient for people trading in Windsor. Merchants kept them in their stores for the accommodation of their customers who did not wish to purchase ten. But the sale of these was stopped. The company, or someone for it, (members of parliament know how these things are managed), secured the services of Col. Beattie, then M.P. for London, to introduce an amendment to the railway-ticket-scalping clause providing that steamboat as well as railway tickets must be bought at the regular offices of the company. This put an end to anyone selling ferry tickets.

Prominent Men You Have Met.

ALDERMAN ARCH. M'NEE.

Arch McNee's continuing fight for the peoples rights gave him the spotlight in the Evening Record *11 July 1907.*
– AUTHOR'S COLLECTION

Col. Beattie had no ferries in his constituency, but he conveniently let himself be used on this occasion. Sir Wilfred Laurier was the only member in the Commons who opposed this amendment, which eventually passed.[11]

In another article, McNee explained that "two monthly tickets had been issued by the company in the past, one, costing $1.00 was good from early morning until 8 PM,

The new ferry boat PROMISE, launched in 1892, fulfilled the company's promise of a modern vessel to replace the aging ships then in service.

    – Windsor Star photo

The Hon. R.F. Sutherland, M.P. for the riding of North Essex and speaker of the House of Commons (1905), was the city's spokesman in Ottawa on the ferry question.
– NATIONAL ARCHIVES OF CANADA, REF PA27974

while the other, costing $1.50, was good anytime. For these two books the company substituted a single book of 100 tickets costing $1.50 good anytime, but very quickly limited their use to the hours between 5.30 & 8.30 AM, 11 AM & 1.30 PM, and 4.30 & 6.30 PM."[12]

Mr. McNee went on to identify some financial benefits the company received from Canada, inferring that in return more attractive fares should be offered to the people: "The company has had generous treatment from this side of the river. Their valuable franchise costs them one dollar a year. The new Ontario Assessment Act has exempted their boats from taxation. Through the efforts of the Windsor board of trade, the government relieved the company largely from the payment of customs officers, for their attendance at the dock on Sunday and at other special times, at an estimated savings of $1,500.00 per year."[13]

Windsor's voice was finally heard in Ottawa. In October 1906 Sutherland forwarded a letter he had received from the Hon. Mr. Templeman, Minister of Inland Revenue, stating that no franchise would be given the present ferry company in 1908, unless they came to some agreement with the city on outstanding issues.[E] If no agreement were reached, the government would "invite public competition for the performance of ferry service".[14] Mr. Campbell was unimpressed with the latest stand taken by the Federal Government. He stood fast in his refusal to meet with city representatives.

In 1907, Arch McNee was an alderman and chairman of the ferry committee. Campbell stood his ground. He would not meet the committee, nor would he see McNee personally. McNee had published one too many articles and letters in the *Evening Record* that were critical of the ferry company and that were in favour of a municipal ferry system. Now that McNee chaired the ferry committee, not much could be accomplished. Speaking of Campbell's refusal to meet with the ferry committee so long as Ald. McNee was chairman, Mr. Sutherland said that he "did not think Mr. Campbell's position was a proper one, neither was it tenable or courteous".[15]

Nevertheless a meeting was finally arranged between the city and the company, for 25 April 1907, in the Ottawa office of the minister of Inland Revenue.[F] The meeting went well for the city (or so it seemed at the time). Templeman the minister re-confirmed his intention to put the ferry franchise up for public tender if the city and the ferry company could not come to an agreement. He also backed McNee's request that a statement of earnings be obtained from the company, which to date Campbell had steadfastly refused to provide. In December 1907, with still no resolution in sight, Templeman stated that public tender would be issued early in the new year. But he failed to follow through with his pro-

---

E   See APPENDIX VI for a copy of the Inland Revenue letter.

F   See APPENDIX VII for the *Evening Record* report of the meeting.

The Evening Record, *as indicated by the cartoon above (16 November 1906), believed that civic ownership of the ferry company was the only way to break the company's monopoly.*

mise, and by early 1908 the city fathers were looking at other means to resolve the impasse. If Campbell would not meet with the committee because of the personalities involved, the city would form a new committee of men who were pro-company. The new committee was appointed (without McNee) in March 1908 "on the pretext that being, as was alleged, personally objectionable to President Campbell of the ferry company, the old committee could accomplish nothing."[16]

Campbell immediately signified a willingness to meet with the new committee, but he firmly refused to meet their demands. The city had met their match. It finally succumbed, accepting the company's terms on 2 March 1908. The terms provided:

1. That books of workingmen's tickets, 100 for $1.50, be sold by the company, good between 5.30 and 9.00 AM, 11.00 AM and 1.30 PM, 4.30 and 6.30 PM eastern time.

2. That in the opinion of this council this class of tickets should not be transferable and that the company should have the right to take up tickets improperly purchased and should have in its discretion to discontinue the sale to offenders.

3. That detachable tickets, ten for a quarter, be sold by the company and that in the opinion of the council the company should be protected in their sale.

4. That the licence be limited to the block from the west side of Ferry Street, to the east side of Ouellette Ave.[17]

The city fathers had ended their dispute with the company by expressing themselves satisfied with the rate and service provided. At the council session of 2 March 1908, they adopted a resolution, to be forwarded to the minister of Internal Revenue, recommending the extension of the existing franchise without any of the concessions formally advocated. Sutherland advised the city on March 30th that Templeman had accepted their recommendations, and that a new lease would be issued. However, the new lease was issued retroactive to 1905. This was probably done to abide by the government's own ruling that ferry leases were to expire after ten years. The previous lease had been issued in 1895. This should have been the end of the dispute, but the company had one more request. They had purchased 300 feet of riverfront property lying between Ouellette Avenue and Ferry Street, and they wanted this extension to their land holdings recognized in the lease. The government readily agreed.

No sooner had this long standing dispute been settled, or forced upon the city as some local residents proclaimed, than another problem emerged. The city and the company were at loggerheads over the dock facilities. The resolution of this conflict would usher in the final phase in the development of the Windsor-Detroit ferry system.

Between 1891 and 1908, four new boats were added to the Detroit, Belle Isle & Windsor Ferry Company fleet. The first of these was the SAPPHO. This ferry was originally purchased by the Walkerville-Detroit Ferry Co. In the closing years of the nineteenth century, it was leased to the Detroit, Belle Isle & Windsor Ferry Company to fill a temporary gap in their capacity. On a summer afternoon in 1901, history was made on the SAPPHO. Theodore E. Barthel drove a gasoline-powered automobile up to the vessel and prepared to drive aboard. According to the local papers, "the captain was beside himself with foreseen dangers. How would the presence of noisy autos affect the horses on the vessel? And what of the possibility of a fire caused by the gasoline carried by the vehicles? The steamer had taken electric cars over earlier, but they were quiet and did not frighten the teams.

Barthel worked for the Oldsmobile Company. They wanted their vehicle tested in Canada so it could be advertised as an "international car". They had approached the ferry company, which initially put up all sorts of red tape, demanding numerous documents to be completed. Barthel arrived with the documents in order, including a bond posted with the customs broker. All went well on the trip. When the auto and ferry safely reached the Windsor side bets were laid by the employees and passengers as to whether the automobile could get up the ferry hill leading to Sandwich Street. Some lost their bets. The automobile made it easily. One outcome of Barthel's trip across the river was a new ruling established by the company that all gasoline automobiles must have empty fuel tanks when boarding a ferry boat. This was one ruling that did not last very long. Everyone saw how silly it was to have to push your auto on and off the boat.

Barthel had a second errand to run that historic day. Another Olds' employee, Jonathan D. Maxwell, asked him to take along some patent applications to Barthel's uncle, Adolph Barthel, who was a patent attorney. Maxwell's patents led to the Maxwell car, a sturdy machine that not only gave the Ford some competition, but provided many funny lines in later years for comedian Jack Benny.

On 21 November 1891, a contract was awarded for a $50,000 steamer to be launched in 1892. Named the PROMISE, this second new boat fulfilled the company's pledge to the public to add a modern vessel to the fleet. Like all new ferries, the PROMISE was primarily used for excursions during her first few years. New and glamorous boats were always a drawing card for the excursion trade.

A story in the *Evening Record*, 5 September 1894, tells of a problem experienced on the ferries peculiar to the age:

Foot passengers normally leave the boat first, before the teams. Today however a horse got restless and bolted, upsetting his wagon and frightening the passengers. The wagon shaft was broken and it will take a ten dollar bill for repairs to the harness and rig. This incident is not uncommon, and people feel horses should be unloaded first as they do get restless waiting.[18]

Apparently the suggestion was accepted by the company. Not much more was written on the subject. In any case, the horse and buggy were eventually replaced by the automobile, which would bring its own problems.

On 30 May 1894, a third new ferry was launched at West Bay City in Michigan, by Wheeler & Company Shipyard. This was the steamer PLEASURE. Company news releases boasted "an interior finish of polished birch, and the main cabin being supplied with many plate glass windows".[19] She had a length of 140 feet, breadth of 39 1/2 feet, and accommodated 3,000 passengers on three decks. This was a far cry from small, single decked-steamers such as the ARGO, GEM or even the FAVORITE. She was dedicated on June 15th, and put into service. Her inaugural trip was an excursion. When the steamer PLEASURE made her first trip from Detroit to Windsor as a regular ferry, an estimated 500 passengers, eager to ride her, rushed the poor ticket takers. All were allowed to board.[20] As soon as she departed the docks a call was placed to the company's office instructing everyone to disembark when the ferry reached Windsor. This was unexpected. The *Evening Record* claimed that "many did not have the nickel for the return fare, having left their home with no intention of spending that much. After a heated debate, however, all were unloaded, and many were stranded on this side while others were only able to return because their lady friends paid their fare."[21]

The fourth and final steamer added to the fleet was the

BRITANNIA, built in 1906. Although the BRITANNIA was used on the Windsor-Detroit run during busy times, and in the winter as an ice breaker, it was primarily built for the Belle Isle run. In 1925, when the Belle Isle bridge was built, the BRITANNIA was refitted as a ferry boat, having one deck removed and a central structure built on the lower deck around which automobiles could move on and off the boat. Most ferry boats had been built with separate cabins on each side of the main deck leaving an area in between for horses and wagons and later automobiles. But this space was insufficient for an automobile, which was unable to turn around and consequently had to leave the ferry in reverse. The BRITANNIA's central cabin arrangement remedied this difficulty. There was enough room for an automobile to drive on to the boat, continue around the circle, and face the gangplank for the drive off. This spacious design was first incorporated into the ESSEX, which was built for the Walkerville Ferry Company, and it was successfully adapted to the BRITANNIA. In her new dress, the BRITANNIA ran as a regular ferry and became a central figure in the cross river commuter scene.

The PLEASURE (1894) was the first ferry capable of carrying 3000 passengers on a single crossing.
– THE GREAT LAKES HISTORICAL SOCIETY, VERMILION OHIO

The city of Windsor (c. 1927). The new docks can be seen at the foot of Ouellette Avenue.
– NATIONAL ARCHIVES OF CANADA, REF. PA48177

CHAPTER X

THE FERRY QUESTION
1908-1928

I beg to advise you that the Detroit, Belle Isle and Windsor Ferry Co. will accept a licence for ten years from the third of October, 1905, and agree to the cancellation of their present licence from that date. The Company will also undertake to continue the present arrangements with the custom officers and maintain all necessary conveniences in the way of waiting-rooms, etc., on both sides of the river during the term of the new licence.[1]

The above is taken from a letter of 22 May 1905, from Walter E. Campbell, president of the Detroit, Belle Isle & Windsor Ferry Company, to the minister of Inland Revenue in Ottawa.[A] A new franchise was due in 1908 , and the city of Windsor was determined to establish a fair passage rate before the lease was issued. They were aware of the poor and outdated conditions of both the vessels and the docking facilities, but the price a passenger had to pay to cross the river seemed to be the real issue. After all, had not Campbell promised to maintain facilities in his letter to the minister?

By 1913 the ferry business had grown significantly, spurred on by an increase in commuters crossing daily to jobs in Detroit, and by the new-found freedom of the automobile. Trips to Detroit to visit the theatre, parks, friends, or just to shop were made even more attractive by the new trolley systems on both sides of the border. Detroiters also crossed in ever increasing numbers to spend time in and around Windsor, including an occasional streetcar trip to the end of Ouellette Avenue, where one could enjoy a day at the racetrack.

Improvements to the ferries and to the Windsor docks, however, had not kept pace with the steady growth in usage.

[A] Around 1912 "Belle Isle" was removed from the Company's name, probably due to the reduced importance of ferry service to the island once a bridge was built. The company became the Detroit and Windsor Ferry Company.

The last boat to be added to the fleet had been built in 1894 and designed for horse-and-wagon days. Except for minor changes and repairs, the docks had not been updated since they had been erected in 1883. The boats did not have the centre island on the lower deck which permitted autos to move in a circle while boarding and leaving the vessel. This would be a feature of later steamers. The automobiles, while "backing" down the passageway, would interfere with the foot passengers and the occasional horse and wagon. Many a passenger had to scurry to avoid being bumped by a passing auto. All of this was brought to the attention of the Windsor City Council, and again they took up the fight, not so much for fares this time – at least initially – as for new facilities.

On 19 July 1913, Campbell took the first step toward improving the situation when he announced that his company was prepared to build new docking facilities at the foot of Ferry Street. They were to be used in two capacities: as auxiliary docks during the busier times of the day, and for the Bois Blanc boats. By November of the same year, the original plans were replaced by an even more ambitious proposal. The company announced that as soon as approval was obtained from Ottawa, a new double-deck dock would be

built that would extend from the foot of Ouellette Avenue to the foot of Ferry Street. The company owned all the land at the foot of both Ouellette Avenue and Ferry Street, but the latest plans called for an extension of twenty-five to thirty feet out into the river bed. "There is an incline to the present table at the foot of Ouellette", Campbell stated, "and the new dock will be carried out on uniform levels to make it easier for teams and autos."[2]

According to the "Navigable Waters Act", the city's Public Works Department could not approve the extension over the river bed without the permission of the federal Marine and Fisheries Department. The company immediately submitted a request to Ottawa, but obtaining approval was not to be an easy task, since various departments from all three levels of government eventually became involved in the issue.

The initial request to Ottawa in 1913 was held up by the city Public Works Department, which wanted time to assess the request. The company was about to obtain the rights to a large piece of valuable real estate right at the foot of Ouellette Avenue in the centre of the city. Once under company control, this property could be used for any purpose, a prospect which naturally did not sit well with the city. Tensions

Author's sketch (from a Border Cities Star *drawing) of the new ferry docks being proposed by the company early in 1924. Similar docks would be built in Detroit to replace those which burned to the ground in 1923.*

were eased when the company agreed to add to any final agreement a clause that stipulated that the property was "for ferry dock usage only". The way seemed clear for the new docks.

Next it was the federal Customs Department which delayed the issuing of the patent. The department wanted assurances from the company that it would provide the necessary customs accommodations and warehousing with the new docks. Someone at a Board of Trade meeting claimed that the Grand Trunk Railway had also raised objections concerning the possibility of the new dock interfering with steamers using its own dock. But the *Evening Record* checked with Ottawa and found that this was not the case.

By March 1916, there was still no action, and people were beginning to ask, "Who is holding up the new dock?" Under its 1905 franchise, the company was obligated to maintain adequate facilities, and indeed it agreed to do so in its letter to the minister. It had not, however, satisfied the customs department, so the order-in-council and the patent were not issued.[B]

Then, in June 1916, a new question was raised. "Is the end of Ouellette Avenue a harbour?" If it were a harbour, there would be no further difficulties, and Ottawa would issue the patent. On the other hand, if it were not a harbour, the province would own the water lots, and the company would have to apply to the provincial government to purchase or obtain a lease on them.

A representative of the Marine and Fisheries Department did investigate, and concluded that the area was not a harbour. The company immediately made application to the provincial Lands and Forests Department. This request was delayed. The city wanted the use of the water lots spelled out in any agreement with the company. Meanwhile, the customs department was still looking for a declaration that their needs would be met. The local Member of Parliament, O.J. Wilcox, assured the customs office that any agreement with the federal government would require the company to provide all necessary facilities. If the company failed to do so, the government of the day would take the appropriate action. This satisfied the customs office, and once again the way seemed clear to begin work on the new docks.

Before any action could be taken by the provincial government, the city repeated its demand that the sale of the water lots be deferred. The dramatic increase in the number of trucks and autos using the ferry had caused considerable congestion in the vicinity of the ferry docks. The city doubted that the proposed improvements to the dock would be adequate to handle the traffic. To overcome the problem the alley running between Ouellette Avenue and Brock Street, just north of Sandwich Street (Riverside Drive today), would have to be widened. This would allow two way traffic and would provide space for customs inspection. To this end, the city council passed a resolution requesting that the federal government purchase forty-five feet of property on the east side of Ouellette Avenue next to the alley. Wilcox responded for the government in a February 1917 communication to the city: "The company had agreed to erect and maintain the required accommodation at this port, and under the law it was necessary for the holder of the ferry licence to provide, to the satisfaction of the minister of customs, a wharf and sufferance warehouse for the temporary storage of goods landed in Canada."[3] Wilcox went on, "It seems to me that the safe course would be to allow the company to proceed with this work, and if upon its completion it should prove inefficient for the purpose for which it is required, the government then would have the same weapon that it has today to force any other action that might be considered necessary or desirable in the public's interest at Windsor."[4] A letter was also received from the Hon. J.D. Reid, Minister of Customs, saying that the purchase of any land as suggested by the council would have to be done through the town's Public Works Department.

The frustrations experienced by the city and the company seemed endless. In March 1917, another incident occurred that forced Campbell to "throw up his hands" and suggest that the company might abandon their plans altogether. Dr. J.A. Smith, the local Collector of Customs, and his superior, Inspector Busby, had taken it upon themselves to investigate the traffic problem. During a meeting with Campbell they strongly hinted that in all likelihood the ferry company would have to purchase sixty feet of property at the rear of

---

B See APPENDIX VIII for *Evening Record* report on the ferry status.

The LA SALLE was launched in 1922 and continued in service until the last ferry ran in 1938.
– WINDSOR STAR PHOTO

the British American Hotel in order to widen the alley. Wilcox was "annoyed beyond measure" at what he regarded as an unwarranted interference on the part of the Customs Department, and he re-iterated the government's position. The March 23rd edition of the *Evening Record* saw all this as a stalemate, and summarized the situation as follows:

> The situation has now come down to this: The city refuses to allow trucks bringing over goods by ferry to obstruct the ferry hill (foot of Ouellette Ave.) and the alley between Ouellette and Brock. The company refuses to go ahead with the building plans. The government is unwilling to buy extra land to widen the alley, claiming that the onus is on the holder of the ferry licence to provide adequate accommodation for a sufferance warehouse.[5]

To muddy the waters of controversy even more, the customs department told the city that "they had the power to stop vehicles anywhere on the street for examination of dutiable goods entering the country. If the city declined to allow this to be done on ferry hill, the customs department would hold the boats for half an hour or whatever time was required, and examine the trucks on board the ferry."[6]

In an attempt to resolve the impasse, the city arranged a meeting at Ottawa, and Campbell was invited. The dispute between the city and the company had been over the question of whether the company had to provide accommodation for teams and trucks after they had passed through the gates of company property but before they had passed through customs. During the meeting, the ferry question was thoroughly thrashed out by the ministers of the departments of the Interior and Customs, both of whom took the view that the company could not be compelled to provide this accommodation. Although the sale of the water lots to the company went through in April 1917 (for $2,000), the ferry question remained unresolved. In 1918, with no solution in sight, the existing ferry franchise expired.

It had now been five years since the ferry company first announced that new docks would be built. The city could not force the federal or provincial governments or the company to insure adequate space for the vehicles leaving ferry property, and individuals and groups were urging the council to approve the company plans and get on with the building of the new docks. When it appeared that the city would finally accept the company's plans for the docks another controversy erupted. On his trip to Ottawa to meet government officials, Campbell had an out-of-pocket expense of $100. Using this rather flimsy pretext, he promptly hiked the rates for autos and trucks by an estimated 30%, and raised the price of passenger tickets by 20%, decreasing the number of tickets, from ten to eight, for 25 cents. In addition, Campbell stated that the 100 tickets for $1.50, good during working hours, would be discontinued. Obviously, the drastic change in the fare structure had little to do with Campbell's Ottawa expenses. He was putting pressure on the city, and the city responded by asking Ottawa to withhold the new franchise until a review of the rate structure could be made. Campbell's reaction to this latest move by Windsor was defiant: "Give us our franchise or we won't build the new docks."[7]

When the existing franchise lapsed in 1918, the company was obliged to operate in the interim under the "Custom's Act." Under this act, all goods entering Canada had to be cleared through customs between nine in the morning and four in the afternoon. In the final analysis, not having a franchise did not hurt the company, whose losses were minimal, or inconvenience the merchants, except for a few market gardeners who simply took their loads to the Walkerville ferry crossing. The company could operate according to the "Customs Act" as long as it pleased.

Now that the initial struggle over the franchise had reached an impasse, the company took a wait-and-see position. The public did not share the company's attitude, however, and pressure was applied to council to drop their objections to the latest franchise proposal. One person summed up the feelings of many when he said, "After all, we are paying 25 cents for 8 tickets now, and Mr. Campbell can change this to anything he wants, for he is no longer bound by any lease agreement for regulation of fares or providing better facilities."[8]

C.R. Tuson, a former mayor of Windsor (1917-18), took

up the challenge. On 27 October 1919, backed by a strong delegation from the Rotary Club and the local Chamber of Commerce, he brought his fight to the council chambers and attempted to convince the council to accept the company's terms. He did not succeed. Mayor E. Blake Winter defeated the move and stated that he "wanted a better deal for the citizens of the Border Cities. This is a matter between the city council and the ferry company to be settled by them without any dictates from any other bodies not elected by the ratepayers."[9] The city wanted the company to enter into an agreement regarding the fare schedule, and it would not remove their objections with the federal government until the company agreed to a change in fares. There the matter ended for the time being.

Campbell turned the screws once again on city council, in December 1919, when he announced that the company was prepared to build two new steamers. Each one would be 170 feet in length and would be capable of carrying sixty to seventy automobiles. They would relieve the bottleneck of traffic, and provide the improved service that the locals desired. But the problem, Campbell stated, "is that we do not have docks in Windsor capable of handling the boats and therefore cannot let the contracts".[10] This proved to be an empty threat. On 29 May 1922, a new ferry steamer, the LA SALLE, was launched at Toledo, Ohio, and early in July it was put into service between Windsor and Detroit. The vessel could carry up to 3,000 passengers and 75 automobiles each trip across the river. The city had the service of a fine new steamer, but the old and outdated dock was congested and inefficient as ever.

The LA SALLE was a functionally designed but beautiful ship. Its three decks glistened in a dress of white, spacious cabins, and polished brass. Along with the CADILLAC (to be built later), the LA SALLE would carry passengers across the Detroit river until the end of the Windsor ferry era in 1938. This is the steamer *we* remember.

Tuson continued his efforts to break the deadlock and is quoted in the *Border Cities Star*, 5 October 1920:

The ferry problem is still with us and apparently no nearer solved than a few years ago. — There is no need of the deadlock that exists between the city council and the Detroit & Windsor Ferry company, and just as long as there is a spirit of stubbornness, so long will conditions become more deplorable. A few years ago the foot passenger, who then received from 7 to 10 minute service, was satisfied, but today he is receiving on the average a 20 minute service, which is very unsatisfactory and means a loss of time waiting at the docks. The automobile service is also disgusting. — The bridge project will never solve the ferry situation as far as the foot passenger is concerned. The people will continue to cross the river at Ouellette Ave. being in direct line with Woodward Ave. and the shortest distance to the business centres. To take a streetcar half a mile down the river, cross the bridge and take a Detroit streetcar to the centre of that city is an impractical thought. In my estimation it will be many years before a bridge is built over the Detroit river.[11]

The franchise standoff showed no signs of letting up and the price of a ferry ride continued to rise, until October 1920, when 25 cents purchased only 7 tickets. Employees' wages were also affected by the squeeze for profits. On 20 June 1921, the company announced a 20% wage reduction for all workers. Council believed that recent progress in the planning for a bridge across the Detroit river (and the adverse effect a bridge would have on the ferry trade) was probably the reason for the wage reduction and the company's unwillingness to agree to a rate schedule. The company, of course, denied everything and assured council that a bridge would not harm the ferry business and that the wage reduction was the result of rising costs.

To break the deadlock, Mayor Winter formed a special ferry committee, along lines similar to the 1908 special committee, which was stacked in favour of the company. Tuson, now an alderman and chairman of the transportation committee, was appointed to the chair of this committee. Formed in early April 1923, the committee wasted no time in coming to terms with the company.

The council met on April 23rd to approve the new agreement. Not all the members were happy. Some felt that the

An early view of the Detroit skyline and the ferry boats BRITANNIA (left) and LA SALLE (right) passing mid-stream.
– A John Boyd photo, National Archives of Canada, ref. PA87073

The ferry ARIEL at the Walkerville dock around 1906.
— Courtesy Don Wilson, Windsor

terms had been dictated to the city by the company. The agreement was to last five years. But there was no clearly stated commitment to provide overnight service or even to extend the present hours of operation. Instead of a promise to hold down fares, the company was given the right to increase them to a straight five cents within the first two years. However, after so many years of delay and dithering, the general feeling among the council members and the public was immense relief. A deal had been brokered – finally!

The debate was not without its lighter moments. Several members were inclined to use biblical metaphors. Ald. A.W. Jackson accused Ald. Tuson of acting as if he were the modern Moses, leading the people of Windsor out of the wilderness of the ferry question. Ald. Roach, who basically accepted the agreement, later stated that he, too, would like to use a biblical illustration and convert some members of the council to his way of thinking. "I could not help thinking," stated Roach, "how St. Paul saw the light on the way to Damascus. Perhaps Ald. Jackson will be as favoured as the apostle."[12]

In the end, Tuson successfully defended his stand, stating that the 1918 council should have struck an agreement but failed. Since that time, the traffic on the ferries had increased. "Thousands of people from Detroit will flock over here to live", he said, "and in a few years this will be a city of one-quarter million."[13] Windsor has yet to reach the 250,000 mark, but in the thick of the roaring twenties, there was plenty of optimism. Council approved the agreement with the company, effectively ending the ferry debate that had lasted for nearly two decades.

Nineteen twenty-three was a banner year for the company: profits were up, the LA SALLE had improved ferry service and now an accord had been reached with the City of Windsor that would pave the way for a new lease from the federal government. The future looked secure. But in the midst of all this positive news the company suffered a great loss. On 7 May 1923, Walter E. Campbell fell ill. Although he appeared occasionally at the company offices over the next few months, his health continued to deteriorate. Campbell and members of the city council were due to meet with government officials at Ottawa to present their joint agreement and to obtain approval for the dock plans. The city waited upon Campbell until August, when it was finally decided that the company solicitor would represent him. The group travelled to Ottawa on August 6th. The federal government approved the plans, and the company announced on August 10th that work on the new docks would commence at once.

For Campbell, it was a Pyrrie victory. On Sunday, September 9th, he died at his summer home on Peche Island.[c] He was a controversial president, who had led the company through the development years since 1891. His loss was felt by friend and foe alike. Following his death, a Detroit *News* article described Campbell in this way:

> Through the years he was in charge of the Detroit and Windsor ferry company Mr. Campbell was totally devoted to his task and he could be found almost daily on the wharves where his boats docked. He was especially concerned for the comfort and safety of his passengers, especially the women and children, and for this reason his boats were always temperance boats. No liquor was ever permitted on his ferries or Bois Blanc boats nor would he permit Sunday dancing on the trips to the islands.[14]

The work on the new docks was delayed again. This time the circumstances were unforeseen. On 28 November 1923, the company's docks on the Detroit side of the river burned to the water with the loss of one life (a fireman). Damage was estimated at $1,000,000. The fire started at three in the morning, originating in an overheated stove in the ferry dock waiting room. It quickly spread to engulf the Bob-Lo docks, the custom houses, and about eight other businesses. The company immediately began ferrying their passengers to the Walkerville Ferry Joseph Campau dock in Detroit, but soon switched to the Belle Isle loading platform, which had been spared by the fire. The fire debris was quickly cleared from the regular ferry docks, temporary offices were built and normal ferry service was resumed. It is interesting to note that the *Border Cities Star* of November 29th reported that while the Joseph Campau docks were being used "many residents of this border who made regular shopping

---

[c] See APPENDIX IX for a news report of Campbell's death.

trips across the river are making many of their purchases on the Canadian side."[15]

To return to the company's plans for new docks in Windsor. The original plans called for two separate docks, one at the foot of Ouellette Avenue, and the other at the foot of Ferry Street, with the controversial coal pile placed in between. (The city had been after the company to remove this unsightly pile of coal since the late 1800s.) But on 14 February 1924, following the fire in Detroit, different set of plans was submitted to Ottawa, calling for a single dock running from Ouellette Avenue almost to Ferry Street. A similar dock would be built in Detroit between Woodward Avenue and Bates Street. Dual docking of boats during rush hours would be possible.

At the time the company unveiled its final plans for the new docking facilities, it announced that it would commission a sister ship to the LA SALLE. Citizens on both sides of the border felt that ferry service on the Detroit river would now be the best offered anywhere. Ald. Tuson was quoted in the *Star* as saying, "The riverfront will be a place of beauty and the docks themselves will be of beautiful architecture."[16]

There is always a construction problem when a new facility is being built on a site in continuous use. So it was with the building of the new ferry dock. In the summer of 1924, the docks at the foot of Ferry Street were partially completed, and the ferry business was moved to these new premises. The workmen then began taking down the old docks at the foot of Ouellette Avenue. Captain Simpson, now president of the ferry company, announced that with the inauguration of the Ferry Street dock a new service would commence. The PROMISE and PLEASURE would provide 10 minute service for foot passengers only. The larger steamer LA SALLE would be given over entirely to the transportation of automobiles. It would provide thirty minute service. In July 1924, U.S. customs personnel were brought aboard the ferryboats, and they processed passengers as they crossed the river. This improved the turn around time at the Detroit dock, and it was hoped that Canadian customs would follow suit. I am unable to locate any record that they did. However, the new dock at Ferry Street seemed to relieve the pressure on the Canadian side. The ferry service was well on its way to fulfilling the expectations of even the most sceptical patrons, and more progress was still to come.

In January 1926, the docks at the foot of Ouellette Avenue were completed and opened for ferry service with little fanfare. The promise of four vessels operating simultaneously could now be realized. The PROMISE and PLEASURE would operate between the Ferry Street dock and the new Bates Street dock in Detroit, maintaining the ten minute service for foot passengers. A new ferry (but not a new boat) would join the LA SALLE on February 10th, to carry automobiles between the Ouellette Avenue and Woodward Avenue docks, providing twenty minute service, which was a real novelty at the time. The BRITANNIA was the name of the LA SALLE's sister ship. Initially it had been built for the Belle Isle run. It had also been used previously on the Windsor-Detroit run, but only sparingly. Refitted, it became a full-fledged ferry boat.

The only remaining construction was to join the two completed portions of the Windsor dock with a common roof and to finish the parking areas and roadways. This was accomplished in the early spring of 1927, and a gala party was held to celebrate the historic occasion. Windsor had finally realized its dream. But the city obtained her new docks and improved service at a steep price.

Even though the steamers were far more powerful than those of the early ferry days, river ice continued to be a formidable foe. It was a rare year when service was not interrupted at least once. The ice could hold fast for days at a time. On these occasions, only a combination of mild weather and the railway ferries would be able to re-open the river to traffic.

On 19 January 1917, the ice caught the PROMISE as well as the PLEASURE midstream, a short distance from each other, and held them fast. Next day the *Evening Record* reported that "four men left the stranded boats, and started for shore, to be helped up at the dock by the people gathered there. Others soon followed, and then the ladies began to take to the ice. Finally a woman carrying a child made the trek, and soon all were safe on shore. Only one man fell through the ice, and only to his waist. He was soon pulled out, and he too made it to shore. The customs people, not to be outdone, were on hand at the dock to check the passengers, and their luggage as they were hauled off the ice."[17] The paper went on to say that "with the ferries unable to run, scores of persons crossed the river ice that night, on foot", and that "next morning three newsboys walked across the river to pick up a supply of Detroit papers, and returned with these to Windsor."[18]

As was often the case during the freeze-ups, the Walkerville ferry was relatively free of ice, and service from there to Detroit continued uninterrupted. Street car service to Walkerville, however, was poor. To assist daily commuters, special "jitney buses" from Windsor to the Walkerville ferry were placed at their disposal.

River ice continued to plague the company until finally, in 1936, it requested permission to withdraw ferry service during freeze-ups. Although travellers now had two other means of crossing the river – the bridge and the tunnel – the city still saw fit to fight the proposal. But, as the end was near for the ferries, the city backed down and the company won again.

It was not just the ice that plagued the ferries. Fog, too, could also cause problems and delays. One rather foggy morning, 17 September 1925, the LA SALLE and the PROMISE were involved in an accident. The LA SALLE was returning from Detroit about 5.30 a.m. when she struck the PROMISE, which was moored just below the regular docks, breaking her mooring lines, and sending her headlong up against a cement wall some twenty yards ahead. The LA SALLE suffered only superficial damage, but the PROMISE, rammed at the stern, was put out of action. Both vessels were immediately tied up for repairs. This left the two remaining active ferries, the PLEASURE and BRITANNIA, to cope with the early morning traffic of six thousand workers going to Detroit. To ease the pressure, the old steamer PONTIAC was pressed into duty, the last time this 1876 ferry would operate on the Windsor-Detroit system. The LA SALLE was repaired without delay. Soon the ferries were operating on schedule.

The PLEASURE fighting the winter ice on the river. The larger and more powerful railway ferries (background) helped to keep the river open by breaking up the ice.
– ONTARIO ARCHIVES, TORONTO, REF. S16276

Walker landscaped the area around his dock and provided an open pagoda where residents could sit and watch the boats, and a green, where lawn bowling was played. The park became known as Riverside Park. Note the steamer ARIEL at dock.
– Windsor Star photo

CHAPTER XI

THE WALKERVILLE FERRY

During the 1830s there was a large scale migration from the eastern United States into the state of Michigan. One of those caught up in the movement was a young man named Hiram Walker (1816-1899), who arrived in Detroit around 1838 and immediately went to work in a local grocery store.[1] Walker was an ambitious man. Before long he had his own general store on Atwater Street near Bates. While this modest enterprise eventually failed, one of Walker businesses that did succeed was the manufacture and sale of whisky in the Detroit area. Unfortunately, Walker's timing was poor. The local temperance movement was rapidly gaining ground, and it directly threatened the production and distribution of hard liquor.

Walker also imported grain. This business took him to the south shore of the Detroit river on many occasions. He quickly recognized the potential of manufacturing whisky in Canada, out of the reach of U.S. regulations, and he set up a distillery on the riverbank just east of Windsor. While whisky remained Walker's primary objective in Canada, he did expand his sphere of business to include homes for his employees, farming, fire and police protection, a church,[2] a bank, and a railway to connect his recently relocated livestock barns and distillery with the Grand Trunk Railway.[3] Soon a small community grew up around his distillery, and it took the name of Walkerville.

Walker continued to live in Detroit, but his expanding interests in Walkerville compelled him to spend more and more time on the Canadian side of the river. Prior to 1890, he was obliged to take a ferry from the Woodward Avenue dock, cross the river to Windsor, and from there travel to Walkerville along the Riverside road. This was a long journey, the last leg of which was extremely uncomfortable because the road from Windsor to Walkerville had yet to be paved with ceder blocks. Furthermore, spring rains turned it into a sea of mud. Walker was one of those nineteenth

Hiram Walker, founder of the
Walkerville – Detroit Ferry Company.
– Hiram Walker Ltd., Windsor

century business barons who would do practically anything to advance his own mercantile interests. To that end, he was generous and imaginative. Weary of his long journey each day, he decided to establish his own ferry service between Walkerville and the east side of Detroit.

The first step was to secure a licence. The Detroit, Belle Isle and Windsor Ferry Company held the franchise for all ferry service between Windsor and Detroit, but this was Walkerville and a different franchise was available. Next, Walker needed the necessary waterfront property for the docks. He already owned the land at the foot of Second Street (Devonshire Road) and he obtained the rights to property at the foot of Walker Street in Detroit. Walker also needed a boat. He went straight to Henry Jenking of the

The ARIEL, shown here in dry dock, was the first ferry steamer built specifically for the Walkerville – Detroit Ferry Company.
– The Great Lakes Historical Society, Vermilion Ohio

The ESSEX (II), named after Walker's first ferry, was the first to load and unload automobiles in a continuous circle around the lower deck.
– The Great Lakes Historical Society, Vermilion Ohio

The SAPPHO was added to the Walkerville and Detroit fleet to replace the original ESSEX.
– The Great Lakes Historical Society, Vermilion Ohio

Detroit Belle Isle and Windsor Ferry Co. His steamer, the ESSEX, had been withdrawn from service in 1878 when Jenking joined the Detroit and Windsor Ferry Association. Walker was able to lease Jenking's boat. In 1880, he commenced his own ferry system. Initially the service was irregular, its primary purpose being to provide for Walker's own travel to and from his Detroit residence. In time, regularity was established, and the ferry company became a proper commercial venture. The new company was called the "Walker and Sons Ferry", and this was changed in 1888 to the "Walkerville and Detroit Ferry Company."[A]

In 1882, the company added a second ferry. Called the ARIEL, it was built by John Oades, whose shipyard was at the foot of Dubots Street in Detroit. The ARIEL was to have a long service record, continuing to carry passengers until it was finally replaced by the steamer WAYNE in 1923. Then it was sold in July to the state of Michigan. The same year the ARIEL was put into service Walker moved his Detroit docks from Walker Street to the foot of Joseph Campau. These docks were used until the end of the Walkerville ferry in 1942. When the ARIEL entered service in 1882, she was placed on a triangular course linking Walkerville, Belle Isle and Detroit. This was a popular move, as it gave the people on the Canadian side of the border direct access to Belle Isle. Walker's ferry company was in business.

Shortly after the ARIEL was launched, a third ferry was acquired. This was the SAPPHO. It replaced the ESSEX on the Walkerville-Detroit run. The ESSEX was subsequently sold by Jenking and used as a ferry between Sarnia and Port Huron. Later on, the ESSEX was destroyed by a fire, a fate suffered by many a ferry steamer, and the long career of a lady that began in 1859 finally ended. The SAPPHO ran for only a short time on the Walkerville run. It was later leased to the Detroit, Belle Isle and Windsor Ferry Company.

After 1900, the automobile industry grew rapidly. It became readily apparent that the ARIEL was not equipped for handling this type and volume of traffic and that a larger vessel would be required. In 1912, plans were drawn up for a new steel ferryboat. This steamer, to be called the ESSEX

after the first vessel of that name, was launched in June 1913, with Mrs. Harrington E. Walker, wife of the company president, performing the honours with a bottle of champagne. Costing in the neighbourhood of $100,000, it had a length of 105 feet and breadth of 36 feet. Her design was new for Detroit river ferryboats, having a centre cabin on the lower deck and an extra wide beam. This allowed automobiles to drive onto the vessel and continue around the deck in a circle, to a point where they could be driven off the boat going forward, not in reverse. This eliminated delays in unloading and reduced the number of accidents. The new ferry had a capacity of thirty automobiles and six hundred passengers. The ESSEX proved so successful that it became the standard by which all future ferry steamers on the Detroit river were designed and built. Indeed, some existing ferries were modified according to her specific design features.

In the ensuing years, two more ferry boats were built for the Walkerville fleet. These were the modern ferries WAYNE and HALCYON. The WAYNE was completed during the winter season of 1922-23 by the Great Lakes Engineering Works in Detroit, and was entered into service on 1 May, 1923. The HALCYON, sister ship to the WAYNE, was built by the same firm. It commenced work in January 1926. After the HALCYON was put on the job, the ESSEX was employed as a relief boat for rush periods or when one of the larger boats was laid up for inspection or repairs

Although the Walkerville and Detroit Ferry Co. shared the same river as the Detroit, Belle Isle and Windsor Ferry Company, it did not share the same problems or limelight. It went along with the crowd, so to speak, and it adapted to prevailing circumstances, avoiding controversy. By 1923, however, the company claimed to be running at a loss of between eight and twenty thousand dollars annually, and asked for new ferry rates to improve their financial position. The Walkerville town fathers agreed, and the order-in-council which had been issued on 20 May, 1920 was amended

[A] The town of Walkerville was incorporated on 5 May 1890. Walker may have anticipated this action when he changed the name of the company.

The WAYNE in her heyday.
– REV. P.J. VAN DER LINDEN,
GREAT LAKES SHIPS WE REMEMBER

The HALCYON was the final boat built for the Walkerville – Detroit Ferry Company fleet (1926)
and for the last few months of operation was the only boat running.
– WINDSOR STAR PHOTO

accordingly. The revised rates were published in the *Border Cities Star*, 17 March 1923:

NEW WALKERVILLE FERRY RATES

Foot Passenger – 6 strip tickets for 25 cents
One seat runabout or coupe and driver 25 cents
Ford touring cars, five passengers and driver 25 cents
Heavy or long wheelbase, under 5 passengers
    and driver 30 cents
Touring, over five passengers and driver 35 cents [4]

The Walkers were proud of their ferry boats, and they kept them in excellent condition. The grounds around the docks were made into a park, later to be called Riverside Park, where Walkerville's "beauty and chivalry" gathered for bowling on the green. There was an open pagoda next to it where the townspeople could sit and watch the lazy river roll by.

The Walkerville and Detroit Ferry Company flourished until it felt the economic pressure of the new bridge and tunnel. It was in the same position as its older downriver rival. The two ferry companies had co-operated throughout the years to their own and the public's benefit. For example, on Saturday evenings during the summer months, the Walkerville ferry would run a special boat from the dock at the foot of Bates Street to their own dock in Walkerville. This special boat gave Walkerville residents direct transportation home from Detroit, a service that was sorely needed, as there were no streetcars running between Windsor and Walkerville at that time of night. The two companies also cooperated in the use of their vessels. If one company were short a boat due to repairs or regular maintenance, they could lease a boat from the other for a day, a week, or even longer.

The automobile played a prominent role in the financial well-being of the Walkerville company. Before final assembly operations were established in Canada, completed vehicles were imported into the country from the United States via the Walkerville ferry. Long lines of new vehicles could be seen at the Detroit dock waiting for transportation to Canada. Loss of this business was one of the contributing factors in the company's decision to discontinue service.

On Friday, 15 May 1942, the company's licence expired. In the days leading up to the expiration, people speculated that that day would be the last day for the Walkerville ferryboats. The company had already retired the WAYNE, keeping only the HALCYON in active service. No official or formal announcement was made. The company did not want to attract the "large milling crowds aboard the HALCYON, tearing off souvenirs, as happened when the Windsor-Detroit ferry service ended four years ago."[5]

It was assumed by the custom officials located at the Walkerville docks, and by the public in general, that the last boat would be at 10 p.m., when the boats normally ended their day. That is why no one took much notice when the HALCYON docked at the Canadian shore at 6pm, and unloaded her few passengers. It did not re-load. The end had arrived. This perturbed the customs agents a little. If they had known, they might have made plans of their own for that evening.

The Walkerville ferry system ended much like this chapter does, with little fanfare, but as the *Star* stated the next evening, "Anyway, that's the way it happened."[6]

A Walkerville – Detroit Ferry Company passenger ticket.
– AUTHOR'S COLLECTION

The HALCYON held fast in the ice just 600 yards from the Canadian shore on 8 January, 1942.
— WINDSOR STAR PHOTO

CHAPTER XII

THE END
1929-1942

Around the middle of June 1938 a "notice" appeared, on the doors and walls of the ferry company offices and on the boats themselves. The notice confirmed what the general public had already gathered from the recent articles in the local papers — that the ferry system was to be discontinued after 18 July 1938. Knowing that the end was near, however, did not lessen the shock and sadness many Windsorites experienced on hearing the official news of the ferries' imminent demise.

"The End" actually began in the teens when the city of Windsor, the higher governments, and the company, were

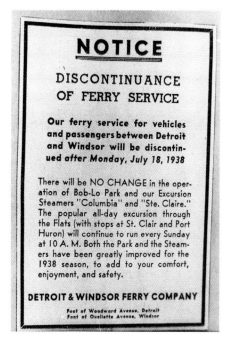

Notice of the closing of the D. & W. F. Co. which was posted at the ferry docks in Windsor and Detroit.

– AUTHOR'S COLLECTION

in continual conflict over dock facilities, boat conditions, fares, and the franchise. Many Windsor citizens thought that the only way out of the "ferry question", was to have one or more levels of government build a bridge or a tunnel. Mayor Winter of Windsor agreed with the public, stating on 20 September 1919 that "a municipally owned ferry system, or a bridge, or a tunnel, is needed to resolve our problems".[1] A few days later he was quoted again. This time he was in despair. He said that "the chance of seeing a tunnel or bridge to connect Windsor and Detroit are, to say the least, remote".[2]

However remote the chances were in 1919, they were a reality a decade later. In 1929, the Ambassador bridge was completed and opened to traffic, and in 1930 the first automobile drove through the tunnel. Originally, the ferry company's management did not fear competition from the bridge because its remote location from the downtown areas of both cities would seem to preclude foot passengers, who had always formed the bulk of their fares. When the bridge was opened on 12 November 1929, however, it was announced that a ten minute bus service would be provided to carry passengers between the two downtowns. The bridge company's fares were competitive too. The pedestrian rate was 5 cents compared with the ferry rate of 5 cents or 25 cents for 6 tickets. A car and driver could cross the river for 50 cents, the same rate charged by the Detroit and Windsor Ferry Company and only 10 cents more than the Walkerville system. The tunnel, which opened in 1930, also provided bus service between the centres of the two cities, at a rate comparable to that of the bridge and ferry companies. The bridge and tunnel provided numerous advantages over the ferries. The trip to the other side was much quicker. There were no problems with winter ice jams. And the usual delays experienced by ferry passengers were non-existent. Any disadvantages were more romantic in nature than practical. Gone would be the leisurely

The WAYNE tied up after the closing of the ferry company in 1942.
– WINDSOR STAR PHOTO

The Windsor and Detroit ferries LA SALLE and CADILLAC (shown above) were the last boats to operate on their system.
– THE GREAT LAKES HISTORICAL SOCIETY, VERMILION OHIO

and relaxing trips across the river. Gone too would be the familiar scene of the steam ferries as they made their way between Windsor and Detroit. More than one hundred years of tradition were about to disappear.

The company was the first to recognize its own predicament. Its days were numbered, despite a few financially healthy months following the opening of the bridge and then the tunnel. But it was not easy to retire from service. There were contracts and agreements to be fulfilled, and employees and shareholders to consider, so the ferries continued long after they had ceased to make a profit for their owners.

After the close of the "Ferry Question", the company continued to operate in a positive manner, upgrading its facilities and boats and maintaining a high level of service to the public. On 11 January 1926, Captain Simpson announced that an extension would be built to the motor car pens at the foot of Ferry Street to allow vehicles to be inspected by customs after they had left the boat. This eliminated delays of up to thirty minutes. The enlarged pens allowed autos to be driven off the ferry immediately upon docking. "In this way," said Captain Simpson, "we will be able to maintain a 15 minute service schedule".[3] This was the very service that Mayor Winter had fought so hard to obtain in 1920. Other changes included overhead loading of foot passengers, who would no longer be required to mingle with moving autos while boarding or leaving the boat.

Upgrading of the docks was not the only step taken by the company to improve its services. It also added a new steamer to its fleet. The CADILLAC, said to be the largest and most powerful ferry on North American waters, was launched 10 March 1928, and was put into service alongside the three existing vessels, the PROMISE, BRITANNIA, and LA SALLE, on April 25th. Capt. Simpson is quoted as saying, "We are adding the new boat so that we can carry automobiles and passengers on four boats at the same time. Boats loading at the foot of Bates Street and Woodward Ave. in Detroit, and at the foot of Ouellette Ave. and Ferry Street in Windsor. One boat will be loading on both sides of the river at all times, and as soon as one leaves a dock, another boat will

slip in and take its place, making the loading of passengers and automobiles practically continuous."[4]

The ferry licence was due to be reissued in 1936. In February of that year, the company applied to the federal government to have the agreement re-written to include a clause that would permit suspension of service between December 1st and March 31st, whenever the company felt conditions warranted such a move. The Windsor City Council, true to form, fought the proposal and asked that the licence not be re-issued. Once again the city and company were at odds, but this time Ottawa agreed with the company and granted the licence with the new wording, on 20 April 1936. Ottawa simply told Windsor that it was unreasonable to refuse the ferry company's request when there were two other ways of crossing the river.

The opening of the tunnel forced the company to reduce their active fleet to two vessels, the LA SALLE and CADILLAC, keeping the BRITANNIA and PROMISE in reserve for emergencies and overloads. Prior to 1930, the four active steamers ran from 5.30 a.m. until 2.30 a.m. the following morning. When the fleet was reduced to two vessels, the operating hours were reduced by two and one half hours, from 6 a.m. to 12.30 a.m. the next morning.

When the end finally came, the first step was to secure the approval of the Interstate Commerce Commission of the United States. Both the ferry company and the tunnel corporation had sustained operational losses since 1930. In a bid to improve its financial picture the tunnel management offered to purchase the ferry franchise. As this move would cancel the ferries, which were a semi-public transportation system, Washington's approval was required. Apparently the ferry company did not require the same permission from the Canadian government in order to cease operations. Therefore, no application was made to Ottawa until after everything had been cleared with Washington.

The tunnel corporation's offer involved $750,000 of new first mortgage bonds and a cash payment of $150,000. In return, the ferry company agreed to discontinue its service and to grant an easement under its properties to the tunnel company. Such an easement would give the tunnel the necessary right-of-way for the construction of a second tunnel, if that ever proved necessary. The proposal did *not* involve the transfer of any of the physical assets of the ferry company. The docks, office buildings, Bob-Lo, and the seven[A] remaining boats would continue to be the property of the ferry company. Nor did the agreement affect the financial stability of the Ambassador bridge or the Walkerville and Detroit Ferry Co. It would, however, affect their volume of business.

On 9 July 1938, Washington's approval was received, and the ferry company officially announced its closing, effective July 19th. Up and down the shoreline, on both sides of the border, the old river mourned. But the sentimental feelings of thousands of people, while genuine, was not enough to save the ferries. Many of these same people had never bothered to use them.

At the time of the closing, the company had two regular ferries running, the LA SALLE and the CADILLAC. On the last day, these two vessels became the centre of merry-making, the likes of which has never been seen on the river since. Angus Munro of the *Windsor Daily Star* was there. Under the headline "HILARITY, TEARS MARK INTERNATIONAL FAREWELL TO OLD-TIME SERVICE", Munro wrote the following story. It is worth quoting in full:

CROWDS INVADE WHEELHOUSE AND KISS CAPTAIN; WHISTLES AND CHEERS SOUND ON BOTH SIDES OF RIVER

Detroit and Windsor citizenry last night paid a hilarious farewell to the ferry service between the two countries when more than 2,500 persons thronged the decks of the good ship Cadillac in her last trip across the historic half mile of water.

[A] The seven remaining boats were the GARLAND, PROMISE, PLEASURE, LA SALLE, CADILLAC, and the two Bob-Lo steamers, STE. CLAIRE, and COLUMBIA.

Never before in the history of the ferry company have such crowds scrambled over the decks of the largest and most modern of the world's freshwater ferries. It was, however, hilarity tinged with sadness at the discontinuance of a servant that has existed for more then a century. The normal capacity of the CADILLAC is 1,400.

From 3 o'clock in the afternoon until past midnight capacity loads thronged the docks and boats making it difficult for the ferry employees to handle them. They invaded the sacred precincts of the captain's bridge and packed themselves into every available space of the large decks and cabins. On the docks they were packed 10 deep in long lines watching for the departure of the boats. Only one ferry was in service in the later hours of the evening.

Capacity loads of automobiles also were a part of the trips from early in the afternoon. Conservative figures of ferry company officials place the crowd that used the service during the afternoon and evening at close to 30,000 persons.

It was entirely spontaneous on the part of the public. They came to bid farewell to the service that carried them to their daily labors for decades. They wanted to be on the last boat and thousands were unable to gain admittance to the gangplanks. So heavy was the passenger load that cars were unable to leave the boat until she was lightened and her lower decks made even with the landing docks.

All formerly rigid rules of the company were broken when adventuresome passengers climbed to the top of the captains bridge and scores rode on the very top of the wheelhouse. Souvenirs in the form of life preservers and other fixtures were ripped from their fastenings and carried away by enthusiasts who wanted a last memento of the trip.

The Detroit – Windsor ferry docks in Windsor about 1937.
  – WINDSOR STAR photo

When the Ambassador Bridge opened in 1929, it provided the travelling public with a faster, and in the winter months, a more reliable means of crossing the Detroit river.
  – WINDSOR STAR PHOTO

The BRITANNIA (foreground) and the LA SALLE waiting for disposition after the closing of the ferry company.
– Windsor Star photo

The CADILLAC tied up at the dock after her final run.
    – WINDSOR STAR PHOTO

The first car through the new tunnel, opened to traffic on 17 October, 1930, was a Chevrolet.
The opening of the tunnel marked the final chapter in the history of the ferry boats.
    – WINDSOR STAR PHOTO

Souvenir Hunters

The souvenir hunters ran rampant throughout the boat. Captain George Waugh reported the loss of his master's license from his cabin. Thirty life preservers were missing from the decks and cabins. Large strips of canvas were ripped from lifeboat covers and anything that was loose or could be wrenched free was confiscated. Not all the collectors were permitted to take their souvenirs off the boat. Many were relieved of their booty at the gangplanks.

Even the fire axes and equipment, locked in glass-covered cases, were prey of the hunters. The crew of the Cadillac removed the cases at last and stored them below for safe keeping.

Sirens and Whistles

The Windsor crowd was equal to that which gathered on the Detroit side despite the big difference in populations. The last boat to leave Detroit was the 11:20 p.m. departure of the Cadillac. As she slowly moved into midstream, auto sirens and ship's whistles were literally tied down and the bedlam ensued for the entire trip across the river.

Navigation was endangered when the press of the crowd made it almost impossible for Captain Joe Mahon to manipulate the wheel of the vessel. On the last trip from Windsor, when the greatest crowd was on board, the Cadillac found it necessary to halt in midstream to allow a huge freighter to pass across her bows. The members of the passenger load had access to the whistle-cord on the upper bridge and used it promiscuously until warned by Captain Mahon that their safety was endangered.

The large vessel, the most modern and finest equipped of the world's fresh water ferry boats, never before carried the load she did on her 11:30 p.m. voyage from Windsor. More than 25 minutes were consumed in the crossing which ordinarily is made in about 10 minutes. So dense was the throng that it was difficult to pass through them from one deck to another without forcing a path.

Old and young alike were in a jovial mood. They sang old songs and shouted farewells as they left the two shores. They refused to disembark at their destinations and the nickel rides that have been the practice of the company for the past few years allowed them the privilege of remaining on board. This resulted in the passenger load doubling itself almost every time the boat docked. There was an unmistakable list to the great, heavy boat as she made the Detroit dock for the last time.

Afternoon Ceremonies

Officially there was no night ceremony planned as all official farewells had been said during the afternoon when mayors of the two cities met on the dock in Windsor and joined hands in bidding a last goodbye to the century-old service. An organized party of the Detroit Business Pioneers and Detroit Old timers made the trip on the 3 o'clock boat and a number of them were in Windsor for about an hour.

"It is just like losing an old friend," Mayor Richard Reading of Detroit declared just before the afternoon departure from Detroit. "I can remember well when as a lad I used to think it a great event to ride the ferries."

George M. Stark, speaking for the Old Timers, recited tales of the old boats that once served the two countries. Black cardboard mustaches adorned the lips of the members of the old timers association as they took part in the ceremony. Mrs. Nelson Clinton, daughter-in-law of Captain William Clinton, known as the father of the present ferry service, spoke briefly of her recollections of her famous relative.

During the afternoon voyage, Captain Henry Pocock, who has served a lifetime in the service of the company and who commanded the Cadillac on her maiden voyage July 20, 1922, was in command. He was relieved in the late afternoon by Capt. Joe Mahon who had the difficult job of handling the night celebrants.

Officials of the company gave up in despair when the overflow crowd spread themselves on the lifeboat decks and entered the wheelhouse to crowd about the helmsman. Down in the interior of the ship where Engineer Joe Walker of Windsor worked his valves and throttles was the only spot on the boat that the enthusiastic crowd did not find access. There they were barred from entrance by the stifling heat of the boilers and the stern warnings of the crew.

Hundreds Cautioned

Employees did a noble job of handling the wildly cheering throng. They warned the hundreds massed on the upper decks to be careful and cautioned the younger lads to stay within safe distance from the unguarded edge of the boat. They were good-natured and amiable despite the dangerous actions of some who insisted on finding new rules to break with each trip.

Police, customs and immigration officers were augmented to handle the dense mass that passed through the turnstiles. Even the usual questioning was reduced to a minimum as the long lines were passed with only one question: "Where were you born?" About 50 government employees on both sides of the river and an equal number of ferry employees will be without duties this morning as a result of the discontinuance of the boats. The two ferries latterly in service. the Cadillac and La Salle were last night tied up with their sister ship, the Britannia. They will be sold, company officials said.

Seated in the more comfortable seats of the boat's large cabin space were many who had used the service for decades. They were not shouting with the spirit of enjoyment that held the crowd outside. Among them were many who carried sentimental recollections of the days when the ferries were the only transportation between the two countries. Not a few showed traces of their feelings.

Tears mingled freely with the cheers that resounded across the water. Old-timers spoke of the days when they made their first trips on such boats as the Victoria and the Excelsior, long since relegated to their marine graves in some neglected dock or sold into other service. Everyone was in a sentimental mood and whether it was gaiety that filled their thoughts or sadness at the last appearance of the familiar boats they were here and there shaking hands with old friends of the old days of the nineties and the earlier years of the present century.

International Noise

As the Cadillac left Detroit on her last trip, the dense crowd on the U.S. side sent up a cheer and the answering whistle of the vessel brought responses from autos parked on both sides of the river and from scores of smaller river craft that slid smoothly through the calm waters of the river. A large golden moon shed its glow across the water to lend enchantment to the scene. It was a night that brought stirring memories of voyages of long ago. The short river trip is always a delight in pleasant weather and nature co-operated fully for the last rites of the famous boats.

As the Cadillac neared Windsor preparatory to docking an answering cheer went up from the Windsor citizens packed along the high wire screening of the docks. They were unable to gain admittance to the boat but they came to join in the celebration anyway. On the loading dock leading to and from the gangplanks, a tightly-packed mob surged and swayed awaiting opportunity to board the boat. More than half were denied admittance so great was the crowd.

The last man to board the Cadillac as she left Detroit on her final voyage to Windsor was Joe Johnson of Windsor who has been an employee of the ferry company for nearly 40 years.

Grew Up With It

He has grown up with the service and it was an eventful trip for him. He spoke hesitatingly of the feeling which he held for his lifetime of service with the river traffic. He smiled as he spoke but beneath his smile one felt the pull of sentiment that must have been his as he gathered his belongings for the last time. Mr. Johnson was a ticket-taker on the ferries when thousands used the service daily.

The last automobile on the boat was that of Charles Wade of 678 Pitt Street west. His car was also the last off the boat at the Windsor dock. On the return trip to Detroit another capacity load was handled.

Throughout the evening rumours spread of many celebrities and near celebrities making the trip. World champion Joe Louis was reported on board the Cadillac but was not located on her last two voyages despite a frantic search by photographer and reporters.

On his last voyage, Captain Joe Mahon was the most harassed man on the ship. Women kissed him and threw their arms about his neck. Photographers flashed bulbs in his face blinding him temporarily until he became alarmed lest he could not see the signals of the river lights so essential to efficient navigation. Ere the mob could reach him as he eased his boat into the dock, he made a quick escape to another part of the ship. He continued to caution the surging mob from blocking his vision as he neared the docks.

BOATS IDLE TODAY

The ferries are no more the servants of a people who have looked upon them as trusted friends, and essential parts of their daily existence. They today are lying idle at the Detroit and Windsor docks, their engines silenced, their familiar crews at home wondering where they will spend the remaining days. They closed an era of transportation in the lives of the two important communities they served. They kept navigation open the year round when, during the winter months, no other vessels attempted to break the ice of the river.

They represent a far advance from the days when Monsieur Leblanc used his rude canoe to ferry passengers over the waters between the two nations by waiting patiently for a fare and being recalled to his home on the Sandwich shore by the sound of a tin horn in the hands of his wife. That was prior to 1820 when the old Argo, the first steam ferry began commercial service between the two shores.

The remaining ferries are in excellent condition. But they have given way in this area to the more modern tunnel and bridge. They have been sacrificed on the altar of progress. Walkerville ferries still continue to operate.

Farewell old friends! You have been good and faithful servants. Your reward is in the overflowing hearts of your former patrons. They will never forget you.[5]

Never again would the trip to Detroit be as pleasant or as memorable as it was on the deck of a ferry steamer. What then happened to last four ferry boats? The CADILLAC, LA SALLE and BRITANNIA became part of the U.S. Coastguard fleet, and the FORTUNE ended up in Sault St. Marie.

The Windsor skyline about 1932. The LA SALLE is in the foreground and the CADILLAC is seen just leaving the Windsor dock.

– AUTHOR'S COLLECTION

CHAPTER XIII

REFLECTIONS

To those who have never crossed the Detroit river on the upper deck of a ferry, the story of the Windsor-Detroit ferryboats will be a matter of history. To my generation, however, the ferry story is more than history, it is memories. But what are ferryboat memories? In my research I asked many senior citizens what they remembered most about the ferry steamers. Strange as it may seem, many people talked about their "experiences in Detroit", and not about the boats or even crossing the river.

The one memory that stood out above all others was "stopping off for a cream ale". In the latter days of the ferry service, Vernors Ginger Ale was produced and bottled in a small plant at the foot of Woodward Avenue in Detroit, next to the ferry company's docks. Inside the entrance there was a "bar" for retail sale of ginger ale "by the glass". This was a beautifully-kept wooden bar, complete with a long brass foot rail. One could order a straight ginger ale, or a "cream ale", a mixture of cream and ginger ale, that was blended just right to please the most discerning palate. This was the most popular drink. Or, one could order a cream ale in one's favourite flavour, vanilla, strawberry, chocolate (I cannot recall all the flavours), but I still remain a fan of the plain cream ale. A unique feature of the sales area was the central purchasing booth. You had to queue up at this booth to buy a ticket for your drink and then redeem the ticket at the bar. A memorable experience for many a traveller returning to Windsor was to stop on a hot summer afternoon for a cream ale before boarding the ferry for home.

Another frequently mentioned memory concerned smuggling. Detroit had large and flashy department stores, such as J.L. Hudson's, Crowley's, and Kerns and Sams, which were always a special attraction for Windsor shoppers. Common wisdom held that any cleverly concealed article would never be detected by customs. I am told that the late Angus Munro once smuggled a long-handled skillet across the border in the seat of his pants, the handle extending up his back. The washrooms on the ferry boats (especially the ladies'), were usually littered with boxes and bags, left by the passengers when they put on their purchases to pass through customs. This type of smuggling was a minor infraction of the law; nonetheless it offered a challenge to many travellers, like the woman who came across on the ferry wearing three dresses over her multiple levels of undergarments.

Smuggling articles across the Detroit river is not a recent invention of today's well-healed traveller or even of the early 1900s. It probably started the day after the United States and Canada created a border between their two nations. By the time the Detroit river ferries had been established in the mid-1800s, smuggling was a tradition, as illustrated in this story from the Detroit *Daily Advertiser*, 25 May 1857.

> We published the remarks of Hon. John Prince, a few days ago in reference to his notice in the Canadian Parliament concerning the Detroit and Windsor ferries. On the following day, as we learn from our Canadian exchanges, the subject was resumed, Col. Prince inquiring of the ministry, as represented in the house, whether it was the intention of the Government to introduce any bill in the present session, for the consolidation of the laws in relation to the ferries within the Province, and also whether the Government has sent instructions to its officer or agent in Windsor, to stop the ferry boats running from thence to the city of Detroit after five o'clock or any other fixed period in the evening; also whether they had issued instructions to any officer to require any person in charge of such ferry boats to make a report or entry at the Customs House in Windsor of each arrival in the day from Detroit to that port; and if so, why such instructions had been so issued.

The Vernors ginger ale outlet in Detroit (lower right), home of the cream Vernors.
– WINDSOR STAR PHOTO

Hon. Mr. Vangoughnet said, with respect to the first inquiry, several municipalities at the border of the lakes had applied to the Government to have a general law relating to ferries established, by which they could manage their own affairs. As to the next inquiry, he acquainted his Hon. Friend that the Government has sent no instructions to stop the running of the ferry in Windsor after five o'clock in the evening. In regard to the last inquiry he would remark that the Government has issued instructions on the 8th inst. to the effect that the person in charge of the ferry should make a report or entry at the Customs House of each arrival in the day from Detroit to Windsor. This was done with a view to protect the revenue; a communication from the office at Windsor having been received by the Government, setting forth that owing to the number of ferry boats the revenue was being defrauded. It was in consideration of this that the order had been issued.

The Windsor Herald says on this subject: "The inquiry of Col. Prince was no doubt, well timed, for it is evident that something had been contemplated in the way of stopping or controlling the ready means of transit which now exists, with a view to the prevention of smuggling. It is our impression that smuggling will receive no impetus by manipulating ferryboats, as those who are determined to violate the revenue laws take a safer means of conveyance than the ferry. If any of the old stagers in smuggling try the regular crossing between Detroit and Windsor, because three boats are running instead of one, they will simply throw themselves into the lions mouth. All of the smuggling that occurs on the boats amounts to a trifle; and it would be looked upon as a act of tyranny if the public were debarred the means of crossing to and fro because a possibility exists that among several hundreds of passengers, perhaps half a dozen pounds of tea, and a like quantity of sugar, might be discovered. In despotic countries the people are under the necessity of waiting to accommodate the Custom House Authorities; in free countries the Custom House Authorities ought to wait

for the people. If they cannot afford to do this, they have no right to fetter the intercourse between two points so nearly allied; where it is well known all have friends on both sides of the river.[1]

In the latter part of the nineteenth century opium smuggling was a common occurrence. The *Evening Record* carried numerous stories of those caught by both the Canadian and US Customs Officers.[2] During Prohibition, "booze" was a likely target, and in the 1930s it was cars and car parts. Today, despite the best efforts of both governments, smuggling continues to be a challenge to the cross border shopper.

Then there were those who spoke about their visits to Detroit's burlesque houses – the National, Gaiety, and Avenue – to the Brass Rail Bar, and to the cigar stores located on the lower part of Woodward Avenue. Some men I interviewed boasted of their exploits at the "shows", while others were too shy to admit anything more daring than strolling slowly past these places, every now and then stealing a glance at the steamy advertisements. They were afraid that someone they knew might see them. Others spoke about trips to La Ford's smoke-shop. One side of the store was lined with barrels of pipe tobaccos, which a customer could mix and blend to his own taste.

For some people, mention of the ferries reminded them of amusement parks, excursions, and moonlight rides. Belle Isle was the first of the "ferry parks" to be opened for the public. It is located on the Lake St. Clair end of the Detroit river. The city of Detroit purchased the island in 1879 from the Campeau family for $200,000, for the "health and pleasure of her people". The Campeaus were the heirs of Lieut. George McDougall who originally purchased the island from the native people. The city developed it into a beautiful park with laid-out drives, lagoons for canoeing, casinos, bathhouses, and boat landings. The island park became an instant success, for it provided just the right setting for youth, families, and courting couples, away from the noise and bustle of the big city. Although ferry service to the island had begun as early as 1851 (a local paper published a notice that the ARGO and ALLIANCE would leave the foot of Woodward for Belle

The original Belle Isle bridge was a wooden structure built in 1889.
– Author's collection

This wooden structure was destroyed by fire in 1915.
– Author's collection

The Bob-Lo boats STE. CLAIRE (foreground) and COLUMBIA about 1980.
– WINDSOR STAR PHOTO

Isle every Tuesday, Thursday, Saturday, and Sunday at 2 o'clock), regular ferry service started when the city of Detroit let a contract in 1883 to the Detroit and Windsor Ferry company. (The name Belle Isle was then added to the Ferry company's name.) The company immediately leased the steamer SAPPHO from the Walkerville and Detroit Ferry Company, and began ferrying passengers to the island. The popularity of the island continued to grow and the company soon found it necessary to use its own boats. In 1892 and 1894, two new boats, the PROMISE and the PLEASURE, were added for the Belle Isle run, easing the pressure on the regular ferry trade. These two vessels would eventually become part of the regular ferry boat fleet, but in the early 1900s they carried many thousands to the park.

In 1889, the first of two bridges was built from Detroit to Belle Isle. It was a wooden structure, which was destroyed by fire on 17 April 1915. It was not replaced until 1917 when a temporary structure was erected. During this period the ferry company continued to bring passengers to the park. However, when the present Belle Isle bridge was completed in 1923, the route became unprofitable and regular service to the island was discontinued.

The Walkerville and Detroit Ferry Company also ran a ferry to Belle Isle for some years, creating a three-point route for their steamers between Walkerville, Detroit, and the island. There are those who recall crossing the river to Detroit on a Walkerville ferry and then walking down Jefferson Blvd. to the new bridge to cross to Belle Isle. Along the way one would pass a very large (about three stories high) replica of a kitchen stove. It was built for the Chicago World's Fair in 1893. After the fair, it was displayed at the Detroit and Michigan Stove Company on Jefferson Blvd. I am wondering if anyone recalls the introduction of the popsicle in the 1940s. They were giving them away free on Belle Isle.

The second amusement park was created by the Detroit and Windsor Ferry Company on an island down river from Detroit called Bois Blanc (Bob-Lo Island).[A] The company purchased the island in 1897. On 20 June 1898, the first excursion left Detroit for Bois Blanc. It is interesting to note

that the company decided not to install electric lights, since it did not want the park to become a "resort for midnight owls". This prudish attitude seems to have continued. In 1913, when the company opened a large and beautiful dancing pavilion on the island, Walter E. Campbell, the company president, announced that he would not allow any "freak" dancing on the floor. To enforce this rule, he placed an officer in charge, who immediately stopped any "turkey trots, bunny hugs, and bear dances". The dancers were restricted to the regulation two-step and waltz, although the "society walk" or "run" was permitted. In fact, most of the couples danced the straight waltz or two-step, "with reverses", and the result was the "best of order and some graceful dancing". As time went on, the company eased these restrictions, little by little. By 1940-41, there was "jitterbugging" every Friday night. The new pavilion had a gallery overlooking the dance floor, to which the public was admitted free. The dancers, though, were charged five cents a couple.

Initially, the company used regular ferry boats for excursions to Bob-Lo. In 1902 and 1910 two new boats were added to the company's fleet exclusively for the Bob-Lo run. These were the steamers COLUMBIA and STE. CLAIRE. Even though the Windsor and Detroit ferry service ended in 1938, these two vessels continued plying between Detroit and Bob-Lo until the end of the regular season in 1991. In November 1991, the Windsor *Star* reported that the COLUMBIA and STE. CLAIRE had been sold to a Chicago based developer L. Spatz.[3]

A third island was purchased by the Detroit and Windsor Ferry Company in 1911, but it was not until 1913 that the company formally announced plans to develop it into an international playground similar to Bob-Lo. The island, Campbell stated, "will cater to the more desirable element of pleasure seekers and the buildings and amusements will be in keeping with this idea".[4] Isle aux Pêches (Peche Island

---

[A] The French name "Bois Blanc" means white wood. The English-speaking public, however, had a problem pronouncing the French name and called the island "Boys Blank". To simplify matters, the company changed the name of their island to "Bob-Lo".

Would you pass the woman on the left through customs? Smuggling has always been a problem on the U.S. – Canadian border.
– WINDSOR STAR PHOTO

Ouellette Avenue looking north towards the ferry docks, taken about 1890. The building on the extreme left housed the post office and customs and is the site of the present post office building.
  – WINDSOR STAR photo

today) never became popular like Bob-Lo or Belle Isle. Walter E. Campbell's summer home was on Peche Island. It was where he died in 1923.

Beginning with the earliest ferries, such as the ARGO and ESSEX, and continuing even today, excursions on the Detroit river have been a popular pastime. They provided a handsome profit for the early ferry operators, but, like the ferry business itself, competition was intense and the ferry captains offered many "extras" to gain fares. Afternoon teas served on deck, local musicians, and special trips to the Sandwich hot springs – these were some of the drawing cards offered to the public. Captain Tom Chilvers of the DETROIT covered the entire upper deck of his vessel with green boughs during one especially hot week in the summer of 1868. This gave the vessel the appearance of a floating tropical island. Under its ample shade passengers could sit and enjoy a gentle breeze as the vessel proceeded along the river. The Detroit and Windsor Ferry Company, along with the Walkerville and Detroit Ferry Company, continued the practice of excursions with regularly scheduled moonlight rides into Lake St. Clair, and day long journeys to the mouth of the St. Clair river. On occasion, they provided special trips for companies, such as Parke-Davis, or the city's merchants. It was on one such excursion that the steamer GARLAND struck the yacht MAMIE, taking sixteen lives.

There were other excursions. Between 1875 and 1887, one of the more popular trips from Detroit was the boat ride to the Sandwich mineral springs, a few miles below Windsor. These springs were noted for their flow of sulphur water, which was supposed to have curative powers. If a silver coin were dropped into the water, it would turn black almost immediately. There were bath houses, eating places, and lounging areas. For a number of years the springs were well patronized, then the flow of sulphur water stopped, and the people left.

About 1885, a George C. Buchanan of Kentucky opened an amusement park on the riverfront just below the springs, and called it Brighton Beach. The ferry boats also stopped there but only for two to three years.

Once upon a time there were ferry steamers sailing across the Detroit river. For a young boy it was a thrill to watch one of those beautiful vessels ease their way into the dock. An employee of the company took your ferry ticket as you entered the waiting area, and unless you hit it just right you would have a few moments to wait for the next boat. For some, this was an anxious time, waiting while the business day slipped by. But for others it was a time to relax and enjoy the sight of the passenger and cargo ships as they made their way up and down the busy river. For the young, equipped with vivid imaginations, the scene provided an endless number of adventures as you sailed to unknown ports and destinations aboard any one of the vessels passing in front of you. Once the ferry boat had docked and the gangplank was lowered, you had to wait a little longer for those on board to disembark, then it was your turn to get on the ferry. Walking across the gangplank always seemed like a ride on one of those moveable floors in a midway show, and it was fun to dart around the older folk, who were taking small steps to retain their balance. Then it was a race for the best spot on the boat. This was high on the upper deck where you could sit at the bow and continue your adventure on the river, perhaps as the ferry boat captain. With a loud blast from its steam whistle, the ferry would pull away from the dock, its decks vibrating underfoot from the powerful engines far below. You would be on your way. If lady luck was with you, one or more large freighters would pass midstream, and you could wave to the deckhands aboard these vessels. But the greatest thrill of all would be seeing one of the legendary steamers, GREATER DETROIT, the WESTERN STATES, or the TASHMOO.

Now with just a few moments left there was time enough to race to the bottom deck and peer through the open doors to the engine room, feeling its blast of hot air and seeing moving parts going every which way. Then back onto the deck again. The trip was over. You heard the loud clanging of chains and the heavy thud of the gangplank being lowered. You reluctantly left your seat at the bow, and climbed down the open stairwell to the deck below to leave the ferry and your adventures. But there was always the trip home.

The passenger steamers have long since departed the scene, but the memory of them lingers on, especially in the hearts of those who rode them. I loved to ride the ferries. I was there that historic day in July when the ferries crossed the Detroit river for the last time. I was aboard the LA SALLE, along with thousands of others. I was being crushed against the wall when a large man picked me up and held me tight, while the merrymakers pushed and swayed to the music. Recognizing the man who was holding me, my aunt held out a piece of paper and asked him for his autograph. He happily obliged. He was Joe Louis, World Heavyweight Champion.

"Once upon a time there were ferry boats."

Season of 1898

MUSIC!

Schremser's 4th Reg Band Orchestra,

On each Belle Isle Park Steamer

EVERY AFTERNOON and EVENING

BOIS BLANC PARK

and AMHERSTBURG.

"STR. PROMISE", daily, 9 a. m., 3:30 p. m., returning 2 p. m. and 8 p. m. FARE—Morning, round trip 35c., afternoon 25c. Sundays 9:30 and 3:30 p.m. Zickels Orchestra. Refreshments. WHARF, FOOT WOODWARD AVE. D. B. I. & W. FERRY CO.

DETROIT RIVER STEAMERS TO BOB-LO   Columbia Ste. Claire (BOIS BLANC ISLAND)

No Draft Permit Required for BOB-LO. No Passengers of Draft age Carried from BOB-LO to Amherstburg Without Draft Permit. Week Days—9 a.m., 1:30 and 3 p.m. Returning Arrive 2 & 8 p. m. Bates St. Dock. Dancing and Bathing. Fare (Except Holidays) 40c Children 25c MOONLIGHT with Dancing on Str. Columbia or Ste. Claire every Evening Except Sun. and Mon. 8:30—Fare 45c. (Except Holidays)

The right to refuse any person admission to boats and park is reserved.

By 1918 the morning and afternoon fares had risen to 40 cents and the island was now called Bob-Lo. Note the reference to the draft permit.
– AUTHOR'S COLLECTION

Columbia Moonlights

Every Tues. and FRI. Eve.

From Foot of Bates St. at 8.30 p. m. Orchestra 16 Pieces. Tickets, 35 cts.

BOIS BLANC Str. COLUMBIA

WEEK DAYS, 8.45 a. m. and 3.00 p. m.   SUNDAYS, 9.15 a. m. and 3.00 p. m. FARE (Round Trip,) 35 CENTS. Str. BRITANNIA Will Make Extra Trip SATURDAY, at 1.30 p. m.

LAKE RIDE—STR. COLUMBIA,

Sunday Evening, 8.30 to 11 p. m. Fare 25 cents. Concert Music—Full Orchestra. Bates Street Wharf. No Liquor.

Moonlight rides too were popular back in 1907 when this advertisement appeared.
– AUTHOR'S COLLECTION

An 1898 advertisement for Bois Blanc Park. Note the morning fare of 35 cents and afternoon fare of 25 cents round trip.
– AUTHOR'S COLLECTION

The Bob-Lo dance pavilion, one of the most beautiful dance locations in North America.
– WINDSOR STAR photo

APPENDIX I

FERRY LEASE TO WINDSOR – 1863

The following is a copy of the ferry lease issued to the town of Windsor by the Province of Canada 1 October 1863. The terms of the lease were written in a very legible hand on a large size parchment.

TEXT OF DOCUMENT

MONCK

Victoria by the grace of God, of the United Kingdom of Great Britain and Ireland, Queen, defender of the faith etc. To all whom these presefts shall come – greeting.

Whereas the municipality of the Town of Windsor, in the County of Essex, hath, under and in pursuance of the forty-sixth chapter of the Consolidated Statutes for Upper Canada, instituted an Act relating to Ferries, applied to us to grant a licence to the said municipality of our ferry or ferries from the said Town of Windsor on the Frontier Line of Upper Canada to the City of Detroit, in the State of Michigan in the United States of America. And whereas, it appearing to us that the said Town of Windsor is incorporated and, as such entitled, under the provisions of the said Act to the said licence, we have assented to the prayer of the said petition upon the terms and conditions hereinafter mentioned.

Now therefore know ye that we do by these presents grant full licence and authority unto the municipality of the said Town of Windsor to establish a ferry or ferries between the said town on the Frontier line of Upper Canada aforesaid to the City of Detroit with power to sub-let the same.

Subject always to the terms and conditions following, that is to say:

First, that all and every such boats and vessels, employed on and used for the purpose of such ferry or ferries shall be propelled by steam.

Second, that the length of keels of all such boats and vessels shall not be less than 60 feet.

Third, that the engine power in all and every such boats and vessels shall be equal to that of at least 20 horses.

Fourth, that the licensee and licenser, and the sub-lessee and sub-lessees respectively, for the time being of the said ferry or ferries, shall at all times during the continuance of this licence, carry over and across the said ferry or ferries without fee or reward, all militiamen, soldiers and sailors, who shall be provided with proper passports, or who shall be with or under the command of their officer or officers.

Fifth, that the licensee and licensees and sub-lessee and sub-lessees, respectively, for the time being of the said ferry or ferries shall obey, observe, abide by, perform, fulfill and keep all such rules and regulations respecting the tolls upon and the attendance at the said ferry or ferries, and the customs and revenue laws of the said province as may in that behalf be lawfully made and obtained.

Sixth, that upon breach of any of the foregoing conditions this licence shall be in the discretion of our governor of the said province cease to exist and become inoperative and void.

Seventh, that it shall be lawful for our said governor-in-council at any time, whenever it shall seem advisable to him so to do, to revoke this licence.

Eighth, that unless revoked or made void the same shall continue over the term or period of 25 years.

In testimony whereof we have caused these our letters to be made patent and the great seal of our said province to be hereunto affixed. Witness our right trusty and well beloved cousin, the Right Honourable Charles Stanley, Viscount Monck, Baron Monck of Ballytrammon in the County of Wexfor, Governor-General of British North America and captain-general and governor-in-chief in and over our province of Canada, Nova Scotia, and the Island of Prince Edward and vice-admiral of the same, etc., etc. At Quebec City this first day of October, in the year of our Lord, one thousand eight hundred and sixty-three and in the twenty-seventh year of our reign.

By command   (signed)   A. J. FEROUSSON BLAIR
                                                    Secretary

APPENDIX II

Copy of the memorial sent to Ottawa to request that the ferry lease be reissued to the town of Windsor (Municipal Archives, Windsor Public Library RG2 BII Vol 1 Clerks Letterbook 1884-1889)

MEMORIAL

To His Excellency the Governor of Canada in Council

The memorial of the Council of the Corporation of the town of Windsor, in the county of Essex and Province of Ontario, respectfully shewith:

1. That the said Corporation has been the holder of a License of Ferry between the said Town and the City of Detroit in the State of Michigan.
2. That the said License was issued under the great seal of the Province of Canada on the first day of Oct., 1863, for a period of twenty five years, and that it therefore expires on the thirtieth day of Sept., 1888.
3. That your memorialists in the early part of the present year took the question of the said Ferry License into consideration, and were advised and did believe that the Act chapter ninety seven, Revised Statutes of Canada was still in full force, and that therefore under section three thereof the license for the said ferry must be offered to public competition.
4. That acting in and upon the belief – aforesaid your memorialists from time to time submitted to the Member for the North Riding of the County of Essex, a series of rules which your memorialists, by reason of their intimate acquaintance with the necessities of the town and county in the matter, deemed necessary to be embraced in the regulations to be established by your Excellency in Council for the governance of the said ferry, with the request that said Member would respectfully present the same for your timely consideration.
5. That today your memorialists for the first time, on the arrival of the Statutes of your Parliament for the year 1888 became aware of the fact that on the twenty second day of May last an Act to amend the said chapter ninety seven was assented to, under the provisions of which "in the case of a ferry between Canada and any other country" the Governor in Council may authorize a ferry license to be granted, or to be renewed for any period not exceeding ten years.
6. That had your memorialists previously known of the passing of the last mentioned Act they would at the earliest possible day have petitioned Your Excellency in Council to grant to the said Corporation a renewal of the said license.
7. That your memorialists regard it as of the utmost importance to this town and county that the control under the license of your

Excellency in Council, of said ferry would remain in the hands of your memorialists – not for the purpose of obtaining direct pecuniary gain therefrom, but because (a) the prosperity and welfare of Windsor and in a less degree of the county in rear of said town, depends to a very great extent upon the effectiveness of the ferry service between this place and Detroit many hundreds of our citizens being employed in that city and must, in order to retain their postions, have both quick and regular service, and (b) because of being on the spot and knowing throughly all the peculiar and special requirements of the public in the matter, your memorialists cannot but believe with all due deference and respect, that they are best qualified to determine the requisite regulations to be observed in such ferry.

Your memorialists therefore humbly pray that your Excellency in Council will not exercise your power under the Act of 1888 to grant a license of said ferry to any individual or private corporation but that you will grant to the Corporation of the Town of Windsor a renewal of the aforesaid license expiring on the thirtieth instant for a further period of ten years and as in duty bound your memorialists will ever pray.

Signed and sealed at Windsor aforesaid for and on behalf of the Council of the said Town this 28th day of September, 1888.

APPENDIX III

Copy of the franchise given to the ferry company by the federal government on 23 August 1895 to expire in 1908.

To all to whom these presents shall come

Know ye that, under and by virtue of the power vested in us in and by the Revised Statutes of Canada, entitled "An Act Respecting Ferries", and the act in amendment thereof and by, and with the advice of the Privy Council of Canada, we have, for and in consideration of the rents, and subject to the provisions and conditions hereinafter reserved and contained and on the part of the lessee hereinafter named their successors or assigns, to be paid, observed, performed and abided by demised and leased, and we do by these presents demise and lease to the Detroit, Belle Isle and Windsor Ferry Co. hereinafter called the lessees, their successors and assigns our ferry across the Detroit river between the city of Windsor, in the province of Ontario, and the city of Detroit, in the state of Michigan, one of the United States of America, to have and to hold the said ferry with all its rights and appurtenances unto the said lessees, their successors and assigns for and during the term of thirteen years, to commence and be computed from the third day of October, in the year of our Lord, one thousand eight hundred and ninety-five, yielding and paying therefor yearly and every year during the said term to us, our successors and assigns, on the third day of October in each and every year, the clear yearly rental or sum of one dollar, the first of such payments to become due and be made on the third day of October, in the year of our Lord, eighteen hundred and ninety-five.

Provided always, and these presents are upon and subject to the provisions and conditions hereinafter expressed and contained, that is to say the limits of the ferry shall from the easterly to the westerly boundary of the town of Windsor as produced to the Detroit river, and a point in the city of Detroit to be fixed by the municipal authorities of that place.

Author's note: The franchise goes on to provide other clauses, one governing the size of the vessels to be used (not less than 85 feet with engines of not less than 100 horsepower), that the company must observe all custom regulations, and that monthly tickets will be issued for $1.00, good anytime between 6 a.m. and 8 p.m.

APPENDIX IV

Evening Record 20 December 1897

THE "MEAL TICKET"

The Disadvantages of the "Ticket" Clearly Pointed Out By The Council

The following is a copy of the memorial passed by the council and forwarded to the Governor-General-in-Council, Ottawa.

1. That on the 23rd August, 1895, Your Excellency's Government granted a lease of the ferry between the City of Windsor and the City of Detroit, for a period of 13 years at the nominal rental of one dollar per annum to the Detroit, Belle Isle, and Windsor Ferry company subject to certain provisions and conditions in said lease expressed.
2. That one of said conditions is that charges for fares on said ferry shall not at any time exceed for foot passengers, 10 tickets for 25 cents.
3. That up to a recent date said company conformed to said conditions and sold 10 tickets for 25 cents, but for a reason believed to be wholly without justification, then refused to sell any more such tickets but compelled patrons of the ferry who do not require a large number of tickets to pay 25 cents for a ticket entitling the holder thereof to 10 passages.
4. Theoretically, this new 10 trip ticket may appear equal in value to the old 10 separate tickets, but practically the two issues are very unequal in value.
5. Under the former practice the head of a family buying 10 tickets was enabled to divide the same among the members of the family, or give them to visitors or other friends, and 10 persons if so disposed might cross the river together on the same steamer. Business men also could and did purchase said tickets for presentation to their customers gratuitously in cases where the customer only desired to cross once or twice.
6. Under the present practice the person buying the ten trip ticket must have the same punched by an officer of the company, causing delay and sometimes the missing of the boat, the latter often a serious matter to such as need to catch a Detroit out-going train, or to reach a factory or place of business at a particular time. In families each member must needs have a ticket, in order to be able to cross the river at will, and this, and in the case of poor persons is a serious tax upon their resources. Aside from the disadvantages mentioned and others that could be urged, the new ticket is clumsy, and easily broken or lost.
7. The said council has endeavoured in conference with representatives of the ferry company to induce said company to live up to the letter and spirit of the said lease, without success and your petition-

ers in response to the urgent demand of their constituents, appeal to you as a last resort for relief from an unjust, arbitrary, and illegal proceeding on the part of said company.

8. That section 10 of said lease reserves to the Governor-in-Council the right "to alter and modify the tariff of charges and tolls" contained therein, should the same "be deemed expedient in the public interest"; and section II thereof reserves the right "at any time at which it may be shown that the lessees have failed to observe, perform, fulfil and keep any or either of the said provisions, restrictions or conditions contained or expressed therein" to declare said lease forfeited and void.

9. That your petitioners submit that said Ferry company have in an important particulars and much to the disadvantage of the inhabitants of Windsor and adjoining municipalities deliberately violated one of the main conditions of their said lease in discontinuing the use and issue of 10 tickets for 25 cents and substituting therefore a ticket of much lower practical value, and thereby inflicted an injury upon the public whose business compels them to use the ferry, and by so doing have invited the penalty provided by said section II of the lease.

Your petitioners therefore pray that your Excellency-in-Council will carefully consider the subject of this petition and take such action for granting the desired relief as to you shall seem meet, not necessarily to the point of forfeiture of said lease, but by compelling the issuance of tickets such as those heretofore in use, and provided for in section 8 thereof.

And as in duty bound your petitioners will ever pray.

Stephen Lusted	John Davis
Clerk	Mayor

APPENDIX V

Evening Record 30 December 1907

PEN PICTURE OF CAPT. W.E. CAMPBELL

Windsor citizens, and more especially Record readers, have heard and read much of Walter E. Campbell, president and general manager of the ferry company, but comparatively few have ever seen the man to know him, and no one has ever seen a full view of his countenance in print from a photo-engraving.

Mr. Campbell dislikes publicity and is as shy of a camera as a March hare is of a hunter.

There are two outstanding characteristics of Mr. Campbell. He is a man of strong personality and extremely frank — even blunt — on his conversation. Courteous usually, but firm.

You could easily imagine such a man sitting as the presiding officer of the board of directors of a large banking institution or mercantile establishment. Further, you would not be surprised if told he completely dominated the whole assembly of directors.

Picture in your eye a man of moderate and medium stature, rather heavy-set frame, iron-gray hair, partly bald in front, and iron-gray mustache. He has piercing dark eyes — orbs that size up things at a glance and fairly beam with shrewdness and intelligence.

When he speaks he can be either affable or abrupt, and even unceremonious. You feel that after he speaks that settles it. His answer is decisive. He means what he says. It is a case of No, with a capital N and a case of Yes, with a capital Y. No half-way measures about President Campbell. No indication of a bluff about him.

"We can't run our boats without making money, and God knows the profit is small enough now," declared Mr. Campbell. That's his answer to the cry for cheaper fares. From the way he said it the answer looked final.

President Campbell, possessing the strong traits of character, as he does, is immune to criticism. As he said at the conference abuse runs off his back as water off a duck.

You almost admire the man for his pluck.

In conclusion, reference should be made to the air of authority in which he moves. For some time before he assumed his present position he was the captain of a ferry here, and he still adheres to the marine power vested in captains.

"Nicholson, stand up and tell us about our theatre experience," commanded President Campbell.

"Botsford, tell us what the figures are on that."

There you have President Campbell. While he is in his present position he is going to run the ferry company to suit himself, and run at a profit.   C.L.B.

APPENDIX VI

Evening Record 19 October 1906

NO FERRY FRANCHISE GIVEN BY GOVERNMENT

Minister of Revenue Says City and Company Must Settle Their Differences or Tenders for Service Will Be Invited

The Hon. R.F. Sutherland has received from the Honourable the Minister of Inland Revenue the following letter, which was handed to City Clerk Lusted. The document, which speaks for itself. will temporarily relieve public anxiety on this very issue:

Ottawa, Oct. 15th, 1906

Honorable R.F. Sutherland, M. P.,
Windsor, Ont.

Sir: In reference to the request of the Detroit, Belle Isle and Windsor Ferry company for an extension for ten years from the 3rd Oct., 1908, the date of the termination of the existing licence, I am instructed by the Minister of Inland Revenue to say that in view of the differences of opinion existing between the company and the city of Windsor in respect to the terms of the license and the manner in which the contract is being carried out the application cannot be entertained. The current licence which expires on the 3rd of October, 1908, the Honorable the Minister holds, should not be terminated by the department on any purely technical ground.

It is further the opinion of the Honorable the Minister that the parties most directly interested, that is the city of Windsor and the ferry company, should come together and settle their differences. Failing an agreement the department will be prepared to invite public competition for the performance of the ferry service between Windsor and Detroit under the terms and conditions to be set forth at the time of advertising, due regard being given to the representations of all parties and beginning on the 3rd day of October, 1908, when the present licence will expire.

Having regard to all the interest concerned and the magnitude of the ferry business at the city of Windsor, tenders (if necessary) should be invited at least twelve months before the date for beginning under a new licence, and as the representative of one of the parties concerned you will see the importance of giving early consideration to the above suggestion.

I have the honour to be,
Sir,
Your Obedient Servant,
W.M. Himsworth
Secretary.

APPENDIX VII

Evening Record 26 April 1907

BATTLED THREE HOURS OVER FERRY QUESTION

Hon. Mr. Templeman Will Apply Screws To Company Unless They Come To Terms With City – Minister Declares That Franchise Will Either Be Handed Over To Windsor Or Held Up For Public Competition.

(Special to the Record)

Ottawa April 26,- The ferry conference with Hon. William Templeman, minister of Inland Revenue, was held yesterday afternoon and lasted three hours. Walter Campbell, president of the company, Capt. Nicholson and Col. N.A. Bartlet, the Canadian solicitor for the company, arrived in time to be present at the conference.

Those who argued the case for the city of Windsor were Hon. R.F. Sutherland, Mayor Wigle, Ald. McNee and Ald. Arnold.

The views of the ferry company were presented by Mr. Campbell, Capt. Nicholson, Col. Bartlet and A.H. Clarke, M.P.

The discussion was carried on in hammer-and-tongs style. From start to finish it was cut and come again.

In a very concise manner, Hon. Mr. Sutherland presented the case of Windsor. He was followed by Col. Bartlet, who tried to excuse the conduct of the company in not meeting with the special committee.

COON COMES DOWN FROM LOFTY PERCH

He said the attack of Ald. McNee on the company was the cause. When Col. Bartlet said Ald. McNee wanted the company to give an account of their business Hon. Mr. Templeman spoke up and asked: "And why not?".

Afterwards Col. Bartlet said the company were willing to give an account of the traffic to the Minister.

Ald. McNee promptly accepted the promise. The delegates regard this as a great victory.

Ald McNee followed Col. Bartlet and in a red hot speech punctured the excuses of the ferry company for not meeting the committee.

"The company gave as an excuse that their Detroit solicitor is out of the city" stated Ald. McNee. Surely Their Canadian solicitors were capable of dealing with a purely Canadian matter. It looks like a reflection upon their Canadian solicitors.

Ald McNee declared the ferry company were only trifling with the letter from the minister and the ferry company.

Before even there was a conference to know what the committee desired, the ferry company refused to meet the committee. Ald. McNee said he had never heard of a company, coming to negotiate for a franchise with a municipality undertaking to dictate what members of the municipality's representatives they would negotiate with.

Ald. McNee gave what he considered many good reasons why the government should restore to Windsor the ferry franchise that had been dishonestly taken from the city. He said the company would not come over to Windsor to confer with the ferry committee, but could come five hundred miles to meet a part of that committee. He urged the minister to tell these people to go home and do as he advised them to do in his letter.

Mr. Campbell, president of the ferry company, followed, speaking in regard to the efficiency of the service and giving a comparison of rates. He said the Belle Isle route did not pay and the company had only recently purchased Bois Blanc park, where all the money came from to establish the fine resort opposite Amherstburg.

Mayor Wigle urged the restoration of the ferry lease to the city of Windsor.

MINISTER HINTED ABOUT CHANGING LAW

A.H. Clarke, M.P., opposed the transfer of the lease to Windsor. He said it was against the present law.

"We can change the law," said Hon. Mr. Templeman.

"Then you would have to treat all ferries alike," said Mr. Clarke.

"I would be pleased to turn over all the ferries to the municipalities," replied Hon. Mr. Templeman.

Ald. Arnold held the documents while the fight went on and did splendid service in prompting the council delegates on the points of the controversy.

Hon. Mr. Templeman said he would be pleased to turn over the control of the lease to Windsor. He would submit the matter to the Governor-in-Council and give the city the answer in a short time. He advised the ferry company to hold a conference with the Windsor council as soon as possible on the question of rates. If the council and the company failed to come to terms he would either hand over the lease to Windsor or put it up for public competition.

The delegates are highly pleased over this decision of the minister. It means that Windsor can still "stand pat" on the matter.

The failure of the company to meet with the ferry committee has injured the company in the mind of the minister.

Mayor Wigle and the ferry company officers left for home last night. Ald. McNee and Ald. Arnold remained over for today.

APPENDIX VIII

Evening Record 16 March 1916

WILCOX MAY SUGGEST GOVT. CANCEL FERRY CO. LICENCE

Dissatisfaction Over Company's Failure To Provide More Accommodation On This Side Growing

The government at Ottawa tells that the Detroit & Windsor Ferry Co. is not keeping faith with the promise to erect new buildings and provide more adequate accommodation on this side.

On May 22, 1905, the minister of inland revenue, received the following letter from Walter E. Campbell, president of the Detroit & Windsor Ferry Co., as now known, which read as follows:

"I beg to advise you that the Detroit, Belle Isle, and Windsor Ferry Company will accept a licence for ten years from the third of October, 1905, and agree to the cancellation of their present licence from that date. The company will also undertake to continue the present arrangements with the customs officers and maintain all necessary conveniences in the way of waiting rooms etc., on both sides of the river during the term of the new licence.

The licence under which the company had been operating was due to expire in 1908, but was renewed for ten years to date from October, 1905. The rent was reduced from $400 a year to the nominal sum of $1 a year. This was done on the representation made by the company that its expenses in connection with retaining the officers of the customs and maintaining all necessary conveniences in the shape of waiting rooms, etc., cost them a large sum.

The holder of a international ferry licence is obliged to observe the following Canadian customs regulations:

The holder of this licence shall provide to the satisfaction of the minister of customs a wharf and sufferance warehouse for the temporary storage of goods landed in Canada from the ferry, and suitable office accommodation for the officers of customs appointed to attend such warehouse.

In 1913 attention was drawn to the department in Ottawa that the traffic on the ferry dock was becoming congested. About this time or a little later it was proposed to extend the ferry landing 20 feet into the river.

The delay is entirely up to the Detroit & Windsor Ferry Co. which has given no reasonable assurance to the customs department that it would put up the necessary warehouses and accommodation. On this account the commissioner of customs recommended to the marine department to withhold the patent.

O.J. Wilcox may suggest that the government cancel the licence and operate a ferry itself as is done between Nova Scotia and Prince Edward Island. The franchise the Detroit & Windsor Ferry Co. has is a very valuable one and it is not believed the company will maintain what appears to be a defiant stand.

Author's note: O.J. Wilcox was M. P. for North Essex.

Border Cities Star 10 September 1923.

FERRY CHIEF PASSES AWAY

Walter E. Campbell Dies At Home On Island

Pioneer Navigator Of River
Was Guiding Hand Of Line Of Boats

Walter E. Campbell, president and general manager of the Detroit and Windsor Ferry Company, died Sunday at his home on Peche Island. Mr. Campbell was 71 years old, and had been in failing health for some time. In the demise of Mr. Campbell, is seen the passing of a pioneer in local marine circles, for apart from holding office as president of the ferry company for more than a quarter of a century, Mr. campbell for years prior to his appointment, was engaged independently in a ferry service between Windsor and Detroit.

BUILT UP COMPANY

Close acquaintants state that the death of Mr. Campbell means the loss of the company's supporting figure. Comments mourning his untimely end were being heard on all sides this morning, for the great development the company had been due to his character, integrity, and energy.

Starting in life as a ticket seller for one of the ferries during the earlier stages of cross river navigation, and later possessing his own boat, the "Fortune" until the ferry amalgamation in 1897, the subsequent career of Mr. Campbell proved to be one laden with far reaching influence.

Ferry enterprises had been a lifelong business with Mr. Campbell. Many persons will recall the Garland, Victoria, Hope, and Excelsior ferries, and the Fortune, the latter which Mr. Campbell owned and operated. It was after the owners of those vessels amalgamated that Mr. Campbell became head of what was then known as the Detroit, Belle Isle and Windsor Ferry Company, a few years ago being changed to its present name.

MAYOR'S TRIBUTE

Mr. Campbell was recognized for his business qualifications throughout all sections of the country, and had given over entirely to the work he undertook in his youth. Mayor Wilson, in commenting on the death of Mr. Campbell today, asserted that the ferry company has lost a great executive, who would be extremely difficult to replace.

Mr. Campbell has been in failing health for a considerable period, but preferred to remain at his Peche Island home rather than jour ney far from the centre of his organization. His friends state that, until the end, Mr. Campbell spared no effort to carry on, and his devotion to his work was perhaps one of the most outstanding characteristics about him.

Since he gained his humble start in an activity that was later to be directed by him, Mr. Campbell always remained one of the most widely known sailors in the great lakes. During the time of the ferry pioneering, he exercised unlimited ability, and carried this through the subsequent years. Always did he have his work at heart, and for years Mr. Campbell made it a point to be at the foot of Bates street, Detroit, at 9 o'clock in the morning, and at 3 o'clock in the afternoon, to order the start of the boat to Bob-Lo Island.

IN RETIREMENT

Socially, Mr. Campbell was of a rather retiring disposition. Owing to his advanced age, and in recent years, failing health, he was obliged to refrain from indulgence in any strenuous recreation, preferring to enjoy the quiet of his Peche Island residence.

While Mr. Campbell's ill-health had been apparent, his death came as a distinct shock to all those associated with him. Locally, Mr. Campbell was known among a large circle of friends, all of whom today testified as to his sterling qualities and manner of leadership in his organization. His death, it is stated in all directions, cannot help but prove a great loss to the community.

Mr. Campbell was a native of Detroit, and besides his widow he is survived by two daughters, Mrs. Stanley E. Vernor, and Miss Esther Campbell. The funeral takes place tomorrow morning at 10.30 o'clock from Hamilton's Chapel, Cass and Alexandrine avenues, Detroit.

CHAPTER	STEAMER	OWNER	BUILT	DISPOSITION
II	ARGO	J. Brutis	1830	Last registered as a ferry 1835
III	LADY-OF-THE-LAKE		1834	Little is known
III	UNITED	L.Davonport	1836	destroyed in a collision in 1879
III	MOHAWK	T. Chilvers	1845	Lost on Lake Huron in 1868
III	ALLIANCE F. BABY		1845	Name chg to UNDINE 1859
II	ARGO II	G. Russell	1848	Retired in 1872
IV	OTTAWA	G. Russell	1852	Leased to G.W.RR 1854
IV	TRANSIT	GWR	1854	Replaced by UNION 1857 Used to ferry cattle until 1867
IV	WINDSOR	G. Russell	1856	Leased to G.W.RR 1856 Burned to waters edge 1866
IV	GLOBE	GWR	1856	Capsized and sunk 1858
V	GEM	W.P. Campbell	1856	Replaced by DETROIT 1864 purch by P.A. Tregeant & Converted to screw wheel tug
IV	UNION	GWR	1857	Taken off ferry run 1874 when RR converted to car ferries, destroyed by fire
V	ESSEX	Jenking Bros.	1859	Sailed until 1880 Sold to Walkerville Ferry Co. 1881 Destroyed by fire
IV	OLIVE BRANCH	W.P. Campbell	1859	
IV	DETROIT	W.P. Campbell	1864	Replaced by FORTUNE 1875 Destroyed by fire at Sandwich dock 1875
IV	GREAT WESTERN	GWR	1866	
V	FAVORITE	J. Horn	1868	Ended her carreer 1873
VI	HOPE	W.R. Clinton G.M. Brady	1870	Replaced by PLEASURE 1894 Sold to Buffalo Group 1895 to serve on the Niagara River
VI	CLARA	W.P. Campbell	1870	
VI	VICTORIA	W.R. Clinton G.M. Brady	1872	
IV	TRANSIT II	GWR	1872	
	MICHIGAN	GWR	1873	
VI	ULYSSES S GRANT	J. Horn	1873	Destroyed by fire 1876
VII	FORTUNE	W.E. Campbell	1875	Sold to group at Sault Ste Marie Mich.
	EXCELSIOR	J. Horn	1876	Name changed later to PONTIAC. The PONTIAC burned at her dock while being converted to a showboat.
VII	GARLAND	J. Horn	1880	Sold to Port Huron group. Name changed to City of Port Huron.
XI	ARIEL	Walkerville	1882	Replaced by Wayne in 1922 Sold to State of Mich. to be used as ferry at the Straights of Mackinac.
IX	SAPPHO	Walkerville	1883	Date is estimate. Vessel later sold to D.BI.&W Co.
IX	PROMISE	D. BI. & W	1892	
IX	PLEASURE	D. BI. & W	1894	
XIII	COLUMBIA	D. BI. & W .	1902	Used exclusively on Bois. Blanc run until 1991.
IX	BRITANNIA	D. BI. & W.	1906	
XIII	STE. CLAIRE	D. BI. & W.	1910	Used exclusively on Bois Blanc run until 1991.
XI	ESSEX (II)	Walkerville	1913	Sold to Imperial Oil Co. ended under Peruvian flag 1948
X	LA SALLE	D. & W. Co.	1922	Sold to U.S. Coast Guard. Scrapped at Cleveland 1951
XI	WAYNE	Walkerville	1923	Sold to Duluth group 1943
XI	HALCYON	Walkerville	1926	Sold to U.S. Coast Guard. Lost off Cape Dorset, Baffin Island 9-15-63
XII	CADILLAC	D. & W. Co.	1928	Sold to U.S. Coast Guard. Scrapped at Hamilton 1952

BIBLIOGRAPHY

Archival Sources

Municipal Archives—Windsor Public Library (Windsor, Ontario)

Unpublished Sources

Hoskins, Ronald G. *A Historical Survey of the Town of Walkerville Ontario, 1858-1922, Including an Evaluation of the Influence of Hiram Walker and His Sons on the Growth and Development of the Town Until 1922.* M.A. Thesis, University of Windsor, 1964.

Newspapers

Border Cities Star (Windsor)
Canadian Emigrant
Courier (Detroit)
Detroit *Daily Advertiser*
Detroit *Gazette*
Detroit *Journal and Michigan Advertiser*
Evening Record (Windsor)
Michigan Herald
Windsor *Daily Star*

Secondary Sources: Books and Articles

Baby, William Lewis. *Souvenirs of the Past.* Windsor: 1896.

Baker, W.A. and Tre Tryckare. *The Engine Powered Vessel.* Gothenburg, Sweden: Crescent Books, 1972: 10.

Cleary, Francis. "The Battle of Windsor". Essex Historical Society, *Papers and Records*, II (ca. 1915): 5-33.

Dictionary of Canadian Biography, XII 1891-1900. Toronto: University of Toronto Press, 1990.

Dowling E.J. "Car Ferries on the Detroit River", (June 1952), *Radio Sketches.* Essex County Historical Society: 1963, 1-4.

Dowling E.J. "Ferry Service on the Detroit River", (July 1951), *Radio Sketches.* Essex County Historical Society: 1963, 1-4.

Farmer, Silas. *History of Detroit, and Wayne County, and Early Michigan.* Detroit: Silas Farmer and Company, 1890.

Haviland, F. "The Detroit, Belle Isle, and Windsor Ferry Co." The Great Lakes Historical Society *Inland Seas* 20:2 (1964): 148-149.

Hilton, George W. *The Great Lakes Car Ferries.* Berkeley, California: Howell-North, 1962: 3-12.

A History of St. Mary's Church, Walkerville 1874-1904-1979. [Windsor: 1979].

Holton, F.J., D.H. Bedford and Francis Cleary. "History of the Windsor and Detroit Ferries". Ontario Historical Society, *Papers and Records* XVI (1918): 40-53.

Hoskins, Ronald G. "Angus Mackintosh, the Baron of Moy Hall". *The Western District: Papers From the Western District Conference,* ed. K.G. Pryke and L.L. Kulisek, 146-59. Windsor: Essex County Historical Society, 1983.

Hoskins, Ronald G. "Hiram Walker—A Man of Two Countries". *Detroit in Perspective. A Journal of Regional History* 2:2 (1975): 97-106.

Jameson, Anna. *Winter Studies and Summer Rambles.* London: Saunders and Otley, 1838.

Lee, Robert E. "The Ten Cent Baby-Sitter", *Detroit Historical Society Bulletin* (March 1966): 12.

Moore, Anna S. "Some Notes on the Argo". The Great Lakes Historical Society, *Inland Seas.* 3:2 (1947): 101-5.

Morrison, Neil F. "The Car Ferries". *Detroit Historical Society Bulletin.* (April 1975): 10-13.

Morrison, Neil F. "The Royal Tour of 1860", (June 1959), *Radio Sketches.* Essex County Historical Society: 1963, 2-3.

Morrison, Neil F. *Garden Gateway to Canada – One Hundred years of Windsor and Essex County 1854-1954.* Windsor: Essex County Historical Association, 1954.

Neal, Frederick *Township of Sandwich. Past and Present.* Sandwich: Record Printing, 1909. Reprint ed. Windsor: Essex County Historical Society, 1979.

Palmer, Friend. *Early Days in Detroit.* Detroit: Hunt and june, 1906.

Palmer, Friend. "Ferry Service Between Detroit and Windsor". *Michigan Pioneer and Historical Collection.* 32, (1903): 463-67.

Quaife, Milo M. *The John Askin Papers, II, 1796-1820.* Detroit: Detroit Library Commission, 1931.

Stimson, M Mansfield. "From Shore to Shore". The Great Lakes Historical Society, *Inland Seas.* 10:3 (1954) 195-205.

Van Der Linden, Peter. *Great Lakes Ships We Remember.* Cleveland: Marine Historical Society of Detroit, Freshwater Press, 1984.

CHAPTER ENDNOTES

CHAPTER I

1. F.J. Holton, D.H. Bedford, and Francis Cleary, "History of the Windsor and Detroit Ferries", Ontario Historical Society *Papers and Records*, XV1 (1918), p. 40. **2.** *Ibid.* **3.** Milo M. Quaife, ed., *The John Askin Papers, II, 1796-1820* (Detroit:, Detroit Library Commision, 1931), pp. 129-130. **4.** Silas Farmer, *History of Detroit, and Wayne, and Early Michigan*, (Detroit: Silas Farmer And Company, 1908), p. 915. **5.** William Lewis Baby, *Souvenirs of the Past*, (Windsor Ont. 1896), p. 14. **6.** Holton, *et. al.*, "History of the Windsor and Detroit Ferries", p. 40. **7.** Neil Morrison, *Garden Gateway to Canada: One Hundred Years of Windsor and Essex County, 1854-1954* (Windsor: Essex County Historical Association, 1954), p. 38. **8.** Ronald G. Hoskins, "Angus Mackintosh, The Baron of Moy Hall" *The Western District: Papers From the Western District Conference,* (Windsor: Essex County Historical Society, 1983), pp. 146-55. **9.** Farmer, *History of Detroit and Wayne and Early Michigan*, p. 915. **10.** *Ibid.* **11.** Friend Palmer, "Ferry Service Between Detroit and Windsor" *Michigan Pioneer and Historical Collections*, 32 (1903), p. 463. **12.** *Ibid.*, p. 464. **13.** Holton, *et. al.,* "History of the Windsor and Detroit Ferries", pp. 40-41. **14.** *Ibid.* **15.** M. Mansfield Stimson, "From Shore to Shore", The Great Lakes Historical Society, *Inland Seas* 10: 3 (1954), p. 198.

CHAPTER II

1. Anna S. Moore, "Some Notes on the Argo", The Great Lakes Historical Society, *Inland Seas* 3: 2 (1947), pp. 101-103. **2.** *Ibid.*, p. 104. **3.** The Detroit *Post*, 7 October 1877, *Michigan Pioneer and Historical Collections,* 2 (1880), p. 580. **4.** Palmer, "Ferry Service Between Detroit and Windsor" p. 465. **5.** *Ibid., Early Days in Detroit,* (Detroit: Hunt and June 1906), p. 79. **6.** Moore, "Some Notes on the Argo", p. 104. **7.** Quoted in Farmer, *History of Detroit and Wayne County and Early Michigan,* p. 916.

CHAPTER III

1. Stimson, "From Shore to Shore", p. 198. **2.** Francis Cleary, "The Battle of Windsor", Essex Historical Society *Papers and Addresses,* II, (ca. 1915), pp. 6 and 10. **3.** Holton, *et. al.,* "History of the Windsor and Detroit Ferries", p. 41. **4.** Cleary, "The Battle of Windsor", p. 8. **5.** *Canadian Emigrant,* 21 February 1835. **6.** *Ibid.*, 13 September 1836. **7.** Holton, *et. al.,* "History of the Windsor and Detroit Ferries", p. 41. **8.** Stimson, "From Shore to Shore", p. 200. **9.** Baby Family Papers, Unit #20-1, sheet 5, François Baby House: Windsor Community Museum. **10.** *Statutes of Canada,* "An Act for better enforcing the provisions of the Act of Legislature of Upper Canada, for the Regulation of Ferries, and for protecting the rights of the Lessees of Ferries", 8 Victoria, Cap. 50, 29 March 1845. **11.** Detroit *Free Press,* 30 March 1859, p. 2. **12.** Morrison, *Garden Gateway to Canada,* p.46. **13.** Farmer, *History of Detroit and Wayne County and Early Michigan,* p. 916. **14.** Palmer, *Early Days in Detroit,* p. 77.

CHAPTER IV

1. Stimson, "From Shore to Shore", p. 201 **2.** N.F. Morrison, "The Royal Tour of 1860", *Radio Sketches,* (Essex County Tourist Association - Essex County Historical Society, Windsor Public Library, 1963), pp. [2-3]. **3.** *Evening Record,* 26 July 1902, p. 8. **4.** Holton, *et. al* "History of the Windsor and Detroit Ferries", p. 43. **5.** Stimson, "From Shore to Shore", p. 202. **6.** George W. Hilton, *"The Great Lakes Car Ferries"* (Berkeley California, Howell-North, 1962), p. 6.

CHAPTER V

1. Holton, *et. al.* "History of the Windsor and Detroit Ferries", p. 44.

CHAPTER VI

1. Allen L. McCrae, "Border Cities Recollections", *Border Cities Star,* 23 August 1919, p. 8. **2.** *Ibid.*, 20 October 1923, p. 3. **3.** *Evening Record,* 1 May 1897, p. 8.

CHAPTER VII

1. The Consolidated *Statutes for Upper Canada,* "An Act relating to ferries", Cap. XLVI. (Toronto: Stewart Derbishire and George Desbarats, 1859), pp. 456-58. **2.** Holton, *et. al.,* "History of the Windsor and Detroit Ferries", p. 46. **3.** *The Evening Record,* 25 July 1912, p. 1 **4.** Angus Munro, "Century of Service on Over-Water Route Terminates Monday", Windsor *Daily Star,* 16 July 1938, Sec. 2, p. 3. **5.** Friend Palmer, "Ferry Service Detroit and Windsor", p. 464. **6.** Municipal Archives-Windsor Public Library, RG 2B II *Letter Book-Town of Windsor, 1884-1889,* p. 387. **7.** *Ibid.*, p. 350. **8.** *Ibid.*, p. 659.

CHAPTER VIII

1. Holton *et. al.* "History of the Windsor and Detroit Ferries", p. 47.
2. *Ibid.*

CHAPTER IX

1. *Evening Record,* 26 September 1906, p. 1.   **2**. Windsor *Daily Star,* 16 July 1938, Sec. 2 p. 3.   **3**. *Evening Record,* 22 September 1897, p. 2.   **4**. *Ibid.*, 25 September 1897, p. 2.   **5**. *Ibid.*, 12 December 1906, p. 1.   **6**. *Ibid.*, 20 October 1906, p. 1.   **7**. *Ibid.*, 26 August 1905, p. 1.   **8**. *Ibid.*, 26 June 1906, p. 1.   **9**. *Ibid.*, 27 June 1906, p. 1.   **10**. *Ibid.*, 26 June 1906, p. 1.   **11**. *Ibid.*, 5 October 1906, p. 4.   **12**. *Ibid.*   **13**. *Ibid.*   **14**. *Ibid.*, 20 October 1906, p. 1.   **15**. *Ibid.*, 24 December 1907, p. 1.   **16**. *Ibid.*, 6 March 1908, p. 1.   **17**. *Ibid.*, 3 March 1908, p. 1.   **18**. *Ibid.*, 9 May 1894, p. 4.   **19**. *Ibid.*, 30 May 1894, p. 4.   **20**. Windsor *Daily Star,* 16 July 1938, Sec. 2 p. 3.   **21**. *Ibid.*

CHAPTER X

1. *Evening Record*, 16 March 1916, p. 1.   **2**. *Ibid.*, 7 November 1913. p. 1.   **3**. *Ibid.*, 13 February 1917, p. 1.   **4**. *Ibid.*   **5**. *Ibid.*, 23 March 1917, p. 7.   **6**. *Ibid.*, 12 April 1917, p.7.   **7**. *Border Cities Star*, 23 September 1919, p. 4.   **8**. *Ibid.*   **9**. *Ibid.,* 28 October 1919, p. 3.   **10**. *Ibid.,* 30 December 1920, p. 3.   **11**. *Ibid.*, 5 October 1920, p. 3.   **12**. *Ibid.*, 24 April 1923, p. 3.   **13**. *Ibid.*, 24 April 1923, p. 3.   **14**. *Ibid.*, 10 September 1923, p. 5.   **15**. *Ibid.*, 28 November 1923, p. 3.   **16**. *Ibid.*, 15 February 1924, p. 3.   **17**. *Evening Record.*, 19 January 1917, p. 1.   **18**. *Ibid.*, 19 January 1917, p. 1.

CHAPTER XI

1. "Walker, Hiram", *Dictionary of Canadian Biography,* XII, 1891 to 1900 (Toronto: University of Toronto Press, 1990), pp. 1097-81.
2. This church should not be confused with the present St. Mary's Church in Walkerville, which was built by Walker's son, E. Clandler. See: *A History of St. Mary's Church, Walkerville 1874-1904-1979* [Windsor: 1979], pp. 7-10.   **3**. Ronald G. Hoskins, "Hiram Walker—A Man of Two Countries", *Detroit in Perspective, A Journal of Regional History* 2:2 (1975), p. 106.   **4**. *Border Cities Star,* 17 March 1923, p. 3.   **5**. Windsor *Daily Star,* 16 May 1942, p. 3.
6. *Ibid.*

CHAPTER XII

1. *The Border Cities Star,* 20 September 1919, p. 3.   **2**. *Ibid.*, 23 September 1919, p. 4.   **3**. *Ibid.*, 11 January 1926, p. 3.   **4**. *Ibid.*, 10 March 1928, p. 1.   **5**. *Windsor Daily Star,* 19 July 1938, p. 3.

CHAPTER XIII

1. Detroit *Daily Advertiser,* 25 May 1857.   **2**. *Evening Record,* Various articles appear on the following dates: 9 February 1893, p. 2, 12 March 1893, p. 4, 22 April 1893, p. 8, 8 May 1894, p. 4.
3. Windsor *Star,* 21 November 1991, p. A4.   **4**. *Evening Record* , 26 August 1913, p. 1.

INDEX

Bold page numbers indicates photo or sketch

INDEX TO FERRY STEAMERS

INDEX TO RAILWAY BOATS

INDEX TO STEAMBOATS